THE FAT MAN'S BOOK

of

STARTERS & SNACKS

by

Tony Grumley-Grennan

First published in 2005

Text copyright Tony Grumley-Grennan, 2005

All rights reserved. No part of this publication may be reproduced, stored in a retrieval system, or transmitted, in any form, or by any means, electronic, mechanical, photocopying, recording or otherwise, without the prior permission of the publisher and copyright holder.

Tony Grumley-Grennan hereby asserts the moral right to be identified as the author of this work.

" The only thing that can be said against eating is
that it takes away the appetite."

The Greedy Book

CONTENTS

FISH BASED DISHES

—

MEAT BASED DISHES

—

EGG, VEGETABLE & OTHER DISHES

—

SELECTION of TAPAS

—

SELECTION of MEZZE

—

SUSHI

INTRODUCTION

This little book is intended as a guide for the preparation of a selection of small dishes that could be used as starters or, indeed, as light meals in their own right. Some of these recipes have been passed to me by friends and relations, most are original but all are easy to prepare and delicious to eat. I have always felt that serving a selection of small dishes like these rather than the ubiquitous starter followed by a main course could make for a fun dinner party, as it does in so many other countries. I have made no concession to fads, fashion or carbo-phobic yuppies and I have ignored all dietary considerations. I have, however, tried to keep it simple. The point is, if I can produce these dishes, anyone can.

The "Larousse Gastronomique", grandly describes *hors d'œuvres* as a means of stimulating the appetite before the main course of a meal, suggesting they should be light, delicate and decorative. It claims that, at dinner, they should be served after the soup course and can be either hot or cold. Amusingly, however, it is an interesting fact that for many years in France, and until relatively recent times, the evening meal consisted solely of soup.[1]

In Scandinavia, which I consider the home of the ultimate snack meal, the *smorgasbord*, which literally means 'table of buttered bread', can either be served as an hors d'oeuvre or a full buffet meal. As a full buffet, the meal can consist of a vast selection of dishes in three or four courses. The first course always consists of various kinds of herring, pickled, smoked or fried, followed by a course of other fish such as, crab, shrimp and lobster salads, smoked fish, salmon roe and caviar, jellied trout and cod's roe. Plates would then be changed again for a third course of cold meats such as pressed tongue, liver pate or a selection of other Swedish charcuterie followed, possibly, by a fourth course of hot dishes such as Swedish meat balls with boiled potatoes and stuffed onions. Crisp rye bread and butter would be served with each course together with the omnipresent aquavit and beer. Each Scandinavian country has it's own version of this meal but it originated in Sweden and dates to the early Norse habit of serving all the dishes for a meal on the table together. A feast in those days was often no more than an excuse to drink vast quantities of alcohol, snack on a selection of fish dishes and end up very, very drunk.

In Russia, small dishes of appetisers known as '*zakuski*' are served to guests prior to dinner together with a glass or two of ice-cold vodka. These hot or cold, small savoury dishes are usually served in a separate room to the main meal. *Zakuski*, although similar to the Scandinavian *smorgasbord*, might also include *piroshki*, small pastries made with puff pastry and stuffed with various savoury fillings such as salmon roe and caviar. Slices of smoked goose, pickled or smoked salmon and trout and sweet and sour pickles of various kinds with black bread and *blinis*, would also be included.

In Indonesia, a meal consisting of a selection of small dishes accompanied by steamed white rice is called a *rijsttafel*, a Dutch word meaning, simply, 'rice table'. There the concept of the hors d'oeuvre has developed into a one-course meal of several highly spiced dishes shared between the guests. There can be as many as thirty different dishes, some hot and spicy, some mild, some dry and others in highly spiced sauces, all accompanied by grated coconut, fried bananas, fried peanuts and various pickles. Apart from a selection of curried meats, there would usually be at least one kind of satay served with a peanut sauce and a spicy sambal.

To countries in the Middle East and the eastern Mediterranean, hors d'oeuvres are known as *mezze* and can be either a selection of dishes at the start of a meal or, again, a whole meal in themselves. There are many different kinds, some simple, some elaborate. Salads, sauces, every type of pickle and dip such as *tahina* and *hummus* make up a selection of mezze seen at every dinner table from Turkey to Morocco and Iran to the banks of the Nile. No Greek meal would be served without *taramasalata*, stuffed *dolmas*, *tzatziki*, marinated olives and a glass or two of ouzo.

Jews across North America, parts of Europe and in particular Britain, have adopted the practice of serving dishes such as *petchah*, *knishes*, *chopped liver*, *gefilte fish*, *gribenes*, *potato latkes*, *schmaltz* and *matjes herring* as appetisers, together with a large selection of pickles. In Poland, as in Russia, Jewish restaurants serve a selection of cold appetisers, with a glass of vodka or schnapps, to customers before they move into the dining room and no formal dinner in a rich Jewish household in Poland would be without a selection of *zakaski*.

In Spain, *tapas* are treated as hors d'œuvres or canapés. The word derives from the Spanish word, *tapa* meaning 'lid' since originally they were slices of bread used to cover a glass of wine to protect it from flies. Today an assortment of *tapas* might be served to accompany an apéritif before dinner. Served in small earthenware bowls or saucers, a selection might include squares of stuffed omelettes, cubes of ham, fried baby eels, snails, fried shrimps and many other delicacies.

Japan has no such thing as hors d'oeuvres or starters as all courses tend to be served at once and eaten in no particular order. Each dish of a Japanese meal is served in individual bowls or platters together with bowls of rice. There are also many one-pot dishes cooked at the table such as *sukiyaki*, *shabu-shabu* and *teppan-yaki* but I have chosen to include a few ideas for preparing *sushi* because they make the perfect starter for any meal.
I wouldn't claim that Chinese *dim sum*, served from trolleys in some of the larger Chinese restaurants, are the eastern equivalent of hors d'oeuvres. *Dim sum* in Cantonese means 'touching your heart' and these delicious titbits tend to be served as a sort of snack mid-morning and are not easy to make. Some can, however, be bought, frozen in most large Far Eastern food shops. Of the hundreds available a selection might include *char siu* (roast pork), *sui mai* (pork and shrimp dumplings), spring rolls, *har gau* (translucent rice flour shrimp dumplings), *fung jeow* (steamed chicken feet) and *fung gau* (translucent rice flour pork dumplings).
Hors d'oeuvres or small savoury dishes should not be confused with canapés. In most countries, canapés are simply various small shapes of sliced bread, fried, toasted or plain, covered with a selection of garnishes such as foie gras, thin slices of ham, mushrooms, anchovies, shrimps, smoked salmon or innumerable other delicacies designed to accompany cocktails or apéritifs.

[1] *Larousse Gastronomique page 999*

CONVERSION TABLES

- Weight -   - Volume -

Ounces	Grams	Imperial	ml
1/4	7	1/4 tsp.	1.25
1/2	15	1/2 tsp.	2.50
3/4	20	1 level tsp.	5
1	30	1/2 tbsp.	7.50
2	60	1 level tbsp.	15
4 oz. or 1/4 lb.	110	1 fl oz.	30
8 oz. or 1/2 lb.	225	1/4 pint	140
12 oz. or 3/4 lb.	340	1/2 pint	280
16 oz or 1 lb.	450	1 pint	560
14 lb. or 1 stone	6.5 kg	1 gallon	4.5 litres

- American Cup Conversions -

1 cup equals

8 oz. or 230 grams of castor sugar
7 oz. or 200 grams of uncooked rice
5 oz or 150 grams of cooked rice
4 oz. or 115 grams chopped onion
5 oz. or 150 grams flour

- Oven Temperatures -

Very slow	110 - 140 Centigrade	225 - 275 Fahrenheit	Gas 1/4 - 1	Aga very cool
Slow	150 - 170 Centigrade	300 - 325 Fahrenheit	Gas 2 - 3	Aga cool
Moderate	180 - 190 Centigrade	350 - 375 Fahrenheit	Gas 4 - 5	Aga warm
Hot	200 - 230 Centigrade	400 - 450 Fahrenheit	Gas 6 - 8	Aga high
Very hot	240 - 260 Centigrade	475 Fahrenheit	Gas 9	Aga very high

Assorted Quotes on Food & Drink

"Never eat more than you can lift."
Miss Piggy

"This recipe is certainly silly. It says to separate two eggs, but it doesn't say how far to separate them"
Gracie Allen

"Part of the secret of success in life is to eat what you like and let the food fight it out inside you."
Mark Twain 1903

"Chocolate is a perfect food, as wholesome as it is delicious, a beneficent restorer of exhausted power. It is the best friend of those engaged in literary pursuits."
Baron Justus von Liebig (1803-1873) German chemist

"People who drink to drown their sorrow should be told that sorrow knows how to swim"
Ann Landers

"I will not move my army without onions."
Ulysses S. Grant, U. S. General

"I often take exercise. Why only yesterday I had my breakfast in bed."
Oscar Wilde

"A gourmet is just a glutton with brains."
Philip W. Haberman, Jr.

"Some people have a foolish way of not minding, or pretending not to mind what they eat. For my part, I mind my belly very studiously, ...for I look upon it that he who does not mind his belly, will hardly mind anything else."
Samuel Johnson

"Once a woman has forgiven her man, she must not reheat his sins for breakfast."
Marlene Dietrich

FISH BASED STARTERS

Most fish have a shelf life of about five days, although in the case of sole, flavour develops when it is stored in the fridge for a day or two longer. Fresh fish, caught the day it is to be eaten, is best for the preparation of *sushi* and *sashimi* and in any event it should have been out of the water for no more than 24 hours. I believe it is almost impossible to undercook fish.

Fish should never be refrozen after having been thawed and is best thawed in the refrigerator rather than at room temperature. Not all fish suffers through being frozen but scallops and other delicate shellfish never taste the same afterwards.
Many of the top superstores now claim to sell good quality fresh and frozen fish in most parts of the country but you can't beat the taste of freshly caught mackerel or freshly picked crab meat on a trip to the coast. It is, however, a sad fact that restaurant food eaten at the seaside often disappoints.

We fear the country's entry into the EEC and the subsequent plethora of laws and regulations controlling fishing and fish stocks, have ruined the British fishing industry and the situation is getting worse. It seems to me one can buy cheaper and better fish in hypermarkets in France these days than in this country.
We buy our fish, however, direct from a Cornish fishing family who sell their catch and sometimes other people's, through their website. It is delivered to us overnight in special containers and is as fresh and delicious as if it had come straight out of the sea. (Details at the back of the book)

Potted Shrimps

There is no point making this delicious starter unless you can get your hands on some of those small brown shrimps found in Morecambe Bay and few other places. They can be bought, frozen in their shells, from good fishmongers but it's worth paying a little extra to buy them shelled. Serve the dish at room temperature when the butter is soft but not melted.

To serve 6
1 lb. shelled brown shrimps
1/2 lb. clarified butter
1/4 tsp. grated nutmeg
Salt & freshly ground black pepper
Paprika

Melt the butter in a bain-marie over simmering water. Flavour with the nutmeg, salt and pepper and add the shrimps. Stir gently for about 10 minutes and then spoon the mixture into individual ramekins, pressing the shrimps down to ensure the butter covers them. Cool and store in the fridge until required. Serve at room temperature, with a shake or two of paprika, a slice of lemon and some fingers of toast.

Tartare of Marinated Salmon

This starter takes some time to prepare but is perfect for a summer lunch or dinner party. It is always better to use wild salmon if you can but, if farmed is all that is available, do make sure it was never frozen.

To serve 8
1 lb. salmon fillet
1 tbsp. each of salt and sugar
1 tbsp. fresh dill, chopped
2 tbsp. Greek yoghurt
1/2 tsp. mild French mustard
Juice of 1/2 lemon
Salt & pepper
Fresh dill for garnish

Skin the salmon and remove all bones. Mix the salt, sugar and chopped dill together and rub into both sides of the fish. Wrap in clingfilm and leave in the fridge for about 10 hours or so. Remove from the fridge when you are about to prepare the dish and rinse briefly under cold running water to remove surplus salt. Dry thoroughly on kitchen paper and chop into tiny cubes no more that 1/8 inch in size and place in a glass bowl. Mix together the yoghurt, mustard and the lemon juice and pour over the chopped fish. Season with a little salt and pepper, mix well and leave to stand until required. Dip a small ramekin in water, shake, and then fill with the fish mixture, pressing it down with the back of a spoon. Invert a plate over the ramekin and gently shake the fish mixture out onto the centre of the plate. Decorate the top with a little of the yoghurt and fresh dill and serve with a slice of lemon.

Fried Scallops

Insist on buying absolutely fresh scallops and those that have not been soaked in water. Soaking in water plumps them up but causes them to dry out quickly when fried, making them tough and unappealing. The best fried scallop dish we have ever tasted was prepared by Shaun Hill when Head Chef at Gidleigh Park Hotel near Chagford. Ask your fishmonger if he can get his hands on any hand-dived scallops rather than those dredged from the sea, many of which may be dead.

To serve 4
16 large fresh scallops
2 tomatoes, skinned, deseeded and chopped
1 clove garlic, crushed
1 tsp. ginger, finely sliced and crushed
1 tsp. garam masala
1 small shallot, peeled and finely chopped
Juice of half a lemon
8 oz coconut cream
Sesame oil
Butter
Salt & pepper

Fry the shallot, garlic, ginger and garam masala for a minute or two in some sesame oil in a small pan, then add the tomato and simmer for a further 5 or 6 minutes. Add the coconut cream and continue to simmer gently. Remove the corals from the scallops and wipe clean, removing any trace of grit or sand. Try to avoid exposing the scallops to water at this stage, but if it is necessary to wash them, do so briefly and pat dry immediately. Cut the scallops in two horizontally and brush the discs with some of the sesame oil and store in the fridge until required. Place the corals in a few drops of water and boil rapidly. Discard the corals and stir the water into the sauce in the pan. Remove from the heat, cool slightly then puree the mixture in a liquidizer and adjust seasoning. Add a knob of butter and the lemon juice and keep warm. Heat a heavy flat-bottomed frying pan until very hot then cook the scallop discs for a few seconds on each side. Do not overcook. They would be just as good raw. Spoon a little of the sauce onto each plate and pile equal portions of scallop discs on each. Serve immediately.
Alternative Instead of the sauce above - try the following, made with frozen peas -
1 lb. frozen peas
1 1/2 oz butter
1 tbsp. sugar
4 spring onions, trimmed and sliced
3 fl oz Greek yoghurt
Salt & pepper

Bring all sauce ingredients to a rapid simmer for 15 minutes until tender. Place in a blender and whiz until smooth, set aside and keep warm. Place a dollop of the mixture on each plate and arrange the scallops on top.

Ceviche

This recipe comes from South America and probably owes its origins to the visiting conquistadors. It is an excellent and easily produced starter. Any white fish will do but it must be absolutely fresh. Avocados also originated in South America and apropos of absolutely nothing, I was told recently that the word, avocado, comes from the Aztec word *ahuacatl* which means 'testicle'. No doubt this refers to its shape and sinful deliciousness. Now isn't that a fascinating thought? Certainly the Spanish Inquisition did their best to ban its cultivation wherever possible.

Serves 4
1 lb. white fish fillets [brill, plaice, lemon sole or flounder], cut into finger lengths 1/2 inch thick
1 onion, finely sliced
8 oz freshly squeezed lemon juice
2 cloves garlic, finely sliced
1 red chilli, deseeded and finely sliced
Salt & pepper
Lettuce leaves and 4 potatoes

Put the fish in a glass bowl. Mix the sliced onions, lemon juice, garlic, chilli, salt and pepper and pour over, ensuring all the fish is covered with the juice. Cover and store in the fridge for 2 to 3 hours. To serve, place a portion of fish on a bed of sliced lettuce with a boiled potato on the side, and sprinkle with a pinch of chilli powder, if desired.

Avocado Stuffed with Ceviche

Take two avocados, cut in half, discard the stones and carefully remove the meat, chop and mix with the ceviche. Add 2-tbsp. olive oil, 2 chopped spring onions and a tomato, skinned, deseeded and chopped. Season well and replace in the avocado shells and serve.

Poached Oysters

People claim that cooking oysters is barbarous. However, we have found that lightly poaching them in a glass or two of white wine makes a most delicious starter. Oysters are saltwater bivalve molluscs found all over the world and have been eaten by man for hundreds of years. The ancient Greeks cultivated them in special beds and the Romans too, ate them in great quantities. Often considered the food of the poor as well as an aphrodisiac they were very cheap and, as a result, were consumed by the barrel load in London during the Middle Ages.

To serve 4
24 oysters, scrubbed clean of grit and shucked
1 onion, finely diced
1/4 pint, dry white wine
3 oz butter
1 tbsp. lemon juice
Sea salt and freshly ground black pepper

Fry the diced onion in the butter until soft, add the wine and heat to a simmer. Season and add the oysters and stir for a few seconds. Pour in the lemon juice and stir gently. Serve in shallow bowls with thin slices of bread and butter

Prawn Toast (Hsia Tui Pao)

Every Chinese restaurant I have been to in Soho serves these simple appetisers. They also make an excellent snack or canapé, dipped in peanut butter or soy sauce.

To serve 8 as a starter or as a canapé at a party
3/4 lb. uncooked king prawns, heads and intestinal tract removed and shelled
1/4 lb. pork fillet, finely chopped
1 cup spring onion or shallot, finely chopped
1 tsp. fresh ginger, finely chopped
1 tsp. salt
1 tbsp. Thai fish sauce
1 tsp. cornflour
1 egg
9 slices 2 or 3 day-old bread
2 tbsp. sesame seeds
Oil for frying

Place all the ingredients except the last three in a processor and mix to a smooth paste. Cut the crusts from the bread slices and spread the mixture on each slice. Shake the sesame seeds over and cut into 4 triangles. Deep fry in batches in the oil until lightly browned. Remove and place bread side down on kitchen paper to drain. Ensure the temperature of the oil remains high enough between batches. They should be served warm with soy sauce or a dipping sauce.

Dipping Sauce
1 fl oz Thai fish sauce
2 tsp. Chinese rice vinegar
2 tbsp. sugar
Juice of 2 lemons, or limes if available
1/2 tsp. chilli, finely chopped

Dissolve the sugar in a small amount of boiling water, [approx. 2 tbsp.]. Add the fish sauce and all the other ingredients and allow to cool before serving.

Grilled Tuna with Avocado Cream

If possible ask the fishmonger to let you have a piece of tuna cut from the fattest piece of fillet he has. It is usually paler than the red meat commonly sold and is much juicier. I always think it a great shame to cook the fish at all as it adds little to the flavour, so ensure it is grilled on all sides for as short a time as possible just to colour the flesh.

To serve 4
1 lb tuna loin fillet
1 avocado
1 large onion, very finely chopped
1 green chilli, deseeded and finely chopped
1 tbsp. dark soy sauce
1 tsp. fresh ginger, finely chopped
Salt and freshly crushed black pepper
Juice of 1 lemon
Sunflower oil

Leave the tuna, wrapped in clingfilm, in the fridge for a few hours to firm up. When you are ready to prepare the dish, remove the tuna, brush with oil and roll in the salt and pepper mixture. Heat a griddle or frying pan until very hot and fry the fish briefly until it changes colour. The centre of the fish should remain raw.
Cut the avocado in half, remove the stone and spoon the flesh into a bowl. Add half the chopped onion, half the chilli, a squeeze of lemon, a drop or two of oil, season with salt and mash the mixture into a thick paste.
Add the ginger, the rest of the onion, chilli and lemon juice to the soy sauce to create a dressing. Cut the tuna into thin slices and arrange on each plate, put a dollop of the avocado paste on the side and spoon some of the dressing over the fish. Serve with a glass of sake or ice-cold vodka.

Gefilte Fish

A famous Jewish dish with many variations. Not everyone's favourite, but the result, I find, is delicious and useful as a stand-by starter or snack. *Gefilte* means stuffed in German and, in the Middle Ages, a forcemeat of chopped freshwater fish was made to stuff pike or carp skins. Nowadays gefilte fish generally means the forcemeat alone, usually made with balls of saltwater fish either poached in fish stock or deep-fried. The fish balls and their juices can be stored in jars for a week or two in the fridge.

For the stock
2 pts. fish stock
8 oz chopped celery
1 parsnip, chopped
1 carrot, chopped

For the fish balls
2 lbs. mixed white fish, [coley, huss, trout, or cod]
2 tsp. salt
1 tsp. white pepper
1 large onion, chopped
2 slices white bread, crusts removed
1/2 tsp. paprika
1 tbsp. sugar
2 eggs

Place the stock in a large pan with the carrots, parsnip and celery and bring to the boil. Simmer for 30 minutes or until the vegetables are soft. Remove the carrots and parsnip from the stock and put in a food processor with the fish, onion and bread and mince until well blended. Add the eggs, paprika, sugar, salt and pepper and blend to a creamy paste. With wet hands, form the fish mixture into small balls, slightly larger than golf balls and gently slide them into the boiling stock, being careful to avoid them breaking up. When all the fish mixture has been used, reduce the heat or remove from the top of the cooker. Cover with a tight lid and leave in a slow oven for 2 hours, carefully turning the fish balls from time to time. Remove from the oven and allow the fish to rest in the liquor for 10 minutes or so. Remove the fish balls, strain the liquor and reduce to use as a sauce. The fish balls can be eaten hot or cold and are best with grated horseradish and beetroot juice mixed together and a little of the cooking liquid, which is called Yuch [pronounced 'yoo-kh']. When cool, store with their liquor in jars in the fridge and serve as and when required.

Gravadlax

I am told the name means *'Salmon from the grave'* in Swedish as, before the introduction of refrigeration, fresh fish was buried in the ground during the winter to preserve it. This ancient Scandinavian delicacy has to be the simplest way of marinating and curing salmon. The result is absolutely delicious, served thinly sliced with mustard sauce and a few slices of brown bread and butter.

To serve 8 - 10 as a starter
Both halves of the thick end of a whole salmon, filleted and boned
A large bunch of fresh dill, finely chopped
For the mustard sauce
2 tablespoons German mustard
1 egg yolk
1 tablespoon lemon juice
Drizzle of good olive oil
1 tablespoon sugar
For the salting mixture
A cup each of salt and sugar

Prepare the sauce by beating together the egg yolk, mustard, sugar and lemon juice and add a drizzle or two of olive oil as you would for mayonnaise. When well blended, fold in half the chopped dill and keep in a sealed jar in the fridge until required. For the pickling mixture, blend together the salt, sugar and the rest of the chopped dill. Lay one piece of salmon in a dish, skin side down and cover the flesh with plenty of the pickling mixture. Lay the other piece of salmon flesh side down on top of the first piece and cover with the rest of the salt mixture. Cover with clingfilm. Place a weight on top and leave in the fridge. After one or two days, most of the salt mixture will have turned to liquid. Remove the fish from the dish, brush off any remaining salt and wipe dry. Wrap in clingfilm until required. Slice the fish thinly, like smoked salmon and serve with brown bread and the mustard sauce as a starter. Mackerel can be pickled in the same way and the mustard sauce is an excellent accompaniment for both.

Prawn Pancakes

These small pancakes can be prepared on the hotplate of the barbecue as you cook your steaks or sausages. They can be as spicy as you wish and, what's more important, can be made with defrosted, ready-peeled prawns although, naturally, raw ones are much better. The pancakes should be cooked very quickly and served as a starter with a squeeze of lemon or a good dollop of mayonnaise.

To serve 4
2 1/2 oz. plain flour
2 1/2 oz. wholemeal flour
8 oz. prawns, roughly chopped
3 cloves garlic, mashed
1 hot chilli, finely chopped
1/2 onion, finely chopped
2 tbsp. parsley, finely chopped
2 tbsp. fresh coriander, finely chopped
Salt and freshly ground black pepper

Blend the two flours together and gradually add some ice cold water until you have made a thick batter. Stir in all the other ingredients and season the batter. Pour some vegetable oil onto the hotplate of a barbecue and spoon the batter on to make small pancakes, about 2" in diameter. Cook on both sides until golden. Serve with a quarter of lemon and a bowl of mayonnaise. If you are not intending to barbecue, the pancakes can, of course, be cooked in a frying-pan in the normal way.

Tony's Stuffed Grilled Baby Squid

The ideal way to cook these little devils is on the hot plate of a barbecue, with a glass of chilled New Zealand Chardonnay in your hand.

To serve 4 - 6
12 small squid [frozen ones from your local supermarket, filleted and cleaned]
3 slices plain white bread
1 onion, finely chopped
4 slices smoked rindless bacon, chopped into tiny cubes
1 garlic clove, chopped fine
1 tbsp. Thai fish sauce
1 tbsp. light soy sauce
4/5 anchovy fillets, finely chopped
1/2 tsp. freshly ground nutmeg
1 egg
1 tsp. hot chilli sauce
Juice from half a lemon
Salt & pepper
12 wooden toothpicks

Defrost the squid and separate the tentacles from the body of the fish. Chop the tentacles into small pieces and set aside. Remove any fins on the body, chop and add to the tentacles. Fry the bacon in a little butter and when nearly cooked, add the onion and continue to fry until softened. Add the squid tentacles and garlic and stir-fry for a few seconds more, then remove from the heat and place in a bowl to cool. Discard the crust then chop the bread finely and add to the bowl, together with all remaining ingredients. Add salt and pepper to taste and mix well. Place the stuffing in the fridge for half an hour or so to allow the flavours to blend. Stuff the squid with the mixture and pin the opening with a toothpick to hold the stuffing in place. Spread a little oil on the hot plate of a barbecue, or in a frying-pan on a cooker, and fry the squid for about 4 or 5 minutes, turning occasionally. Do not overcook.
Remove the toothpicks and serve as a starter, with a squeeze of lemon and a green salad.

Haddock Brandade with Scallops

Traditional brandade is made from smoked cod, garlic and cream but haddock works just as well and is more easily found. A poached egg instead of the scallops is another option.

To serve 4
8 oz. smoked haddock, undyed
8 oz. mashed potato
2 cloves garlic, finely chopped
1/2 pint milk
3 tbsp. double cream
juice of 1/2 lemon
1 oz. Cheddar cheese, grated
6 scallops
Selection of salad leaves
Olive oil and balsamic vinegar dressing
Salt and freshly ground black pepper

Place the haddock, garlic and milk on low heat and slowly bring to the boil. Remove the pan from the heat, cover with a lid and leave to stand and cool. When cool enough to handle, drain the fish and discard the garlic and milk. Skin the fish and flake the flesh into a bowl, being careful to remove any small bones. Mix the mashed potato, flaked fish, cream, lemon juice and cheese and season with a twist or two of salt and freshly ground black pepper. Remove and discard the coral and slice the scallops in half. Pour a drop of oil into a non-stick frying pan on high heat and sear the scallops on each side. Do not overcook as they will become very chewy. Scatter a few salad leaves on each plate, make a dressing with the oil and balsamic vinegar and dress the salad leaves. Divide the brandade between each plate and place three pieces of scallop on top. Serve immediately. If scallops are too expensive or are unobtainable, poach 4 eggs and place them on top instead.

Fish Terrine

This recipe requires fillets of three different fish. It is
easy to make, takes no time to prepare and can be made
in advance and stored, covered, in the fridge until required.

To serve 6 - 8
8 oz. fillets of coley, skinned
8 oz. fillets of fresh salmon, skinned
8 oz. fillets of monkfish tail, boned and skinned
4 egg whites, beaten until stiff
1 pint, double cream
1/2 tsp. turmeric powder
1 tbsp. dill, finely chopped
Good handfull of parsley, finely chopped
Salt & freshly ground black pepper

Blend each portion of fish separately in a food processor with a third of the cream and a third of the egg whites, season well and set aside. Add chopped parsley to the coley mixture, turmeric to the monkfish mixture and dill to the salmon. Grease the bottom and sides of a suitable terrine and fill with alternate layers of the fish. Cook in a medium oven in a bain-marie for an hour. Allow the terrine to stand for 10 minutes or so before carefully tipping it onto a suitable serving dish. It is best served warm with a glass of dry sherry and slices of brown bread and butter.

Smoked Mackerel & Horseradish Pate

A friend, Mary Rose, found this recipe and we have experimented with it using
different ingredients. However, we believe that the original recipe she produced
at a recent supper, cannot be bettered. Nevertheless, those concerned about the
richness of the dish might wish to try Greek yoghurt as an alternative to cream.

To serve 4 - 6
10 oz. smoked mackerel fillets (plain or peppered)
2 oz. unsalted butter
3 tbsp. creamed horseradish
2 tbsp. double cream
Freshly ground black pepper

Combine all the ingredients in a blender and season well. Check consistency and flavour and add more cream, if desired. Spoon into a small dish or a series of ramekins, chill and serve with triangles of warm toast.

Escabeche (Pickled Fried Fish)

Escabeche, from the medieval Arabic word, *sikbaj*, meaning sour,
is a recipe for preparing and preserving small fish or fish fillets.
The dish may have originated in Portugal or Spain and is also found
in South America and North Africa. Choose the biggest and fattest
herring you can find, assuming they haven't all been sold on the continent!

For storing in the fridge
6 large herring, filleted
8 fl oz white wine vinegar
4 fl oz water
1 small onion, finely sliced
1 small carrot, finely diced
3 tbsp. vegetable oil
3 cloves garlic, chopped extremely finely or squashed
Selection of whole spices to include - 1 bay leaf, 1 tsp. each allspice, peppercorns, cloves
1/4 tsp. ground mace or nutmeg
3 or 4 sprigs of parsley
Flour, seasoned with salt, pepper and a pinch of ground chilli

Dredge the fish fillets in the flour mixture, shaking off any surplus. Fry briefly in the oil until golden on both sides, remove with a slotted spoon and drain on kitchen paper. Place them in a deep ceramic dish. Fry the onion, carrot and garlic until they begin to colour then add all the other ingredients. Heat through and pour over the fish. Allow to cool, cover and keep in the fridge for a couple of days for the flavours to blend. Perfect served as a starter with hunks of freshly-baked wholemeal bread or a small boiled potato and sour cream.

Potted Salmon

Try to find fresh wild salmon for this recipe as it tends to taste so much better. Should the fresh wild salmon be too expensive or hard to find, try wild sea trout instead.

To serve 8
2 lb. salmon fillet, boned and skinned
10 oz. butter
2 tbsp. olive oil
Juice of 2 lemons
2 tsp. salt
1 or 2 drops of chilli or Worcestershire sauce
Freshly ground black pepper

Bring 1/2 pint of water to the boil, add the lemon juice and salt and simmer gently. Add the salmon and cook, covered, for five minutes or so. Remove from the heat and allow the fish to cool in the water. When the fish is cool enough to handle, flake it into individual ramekins, taking care to remove any remaining skin or bones. Heat the butter to simmering point and clarify it by straining it through a fine sieve. Add the oil and chilli sauce, season well and simmer over low heat, stirring constantly. Pour the butter over the fish in each ramekin ensuring the fish is well covered, cool and store in the fridge until required and serve with slices of toast and a quarter of lemon.

Salmon Rillettes

Pieces of shredded pork, rabbit or goose flesh, slow cooked in fat, are the normal ingredients used to make rillette but fresh or smoked salmon makes a fine alternative.

To make a 1 lb jar of paste.
1 lb. salmon, skinned and boned
4 oz. butter
1 small onion, skinned and very finely chopped
1 tbsp. Greek yoghurt
8 oz. chunk of smoked salmon, diced
2 tbsp. lemon juice
1 tbsp. olive oil
2 egg yolks, lightly beaten
Salt and freshly ground black pepper

Season the salmon on all sides and place in a dish in the fridge for an hour or so to marinate. Then place the salmon in a steamer, cover and steam gently for seven or eight minutes. Fry the onions in butter until soft but not browned, season and mix in the poached salmon in chunks and the smoked salmon cubes. Beat the Greek yoghurt and remaining butter together with the lemon juice, olive oil and egg yolks and fold into the fish mixture. Put the mixture into a large sealed jar and cover with a layer of melted butter. Serve with pieces of fresh toasted bread and pickles.

Creamed Crab & Avocado

This recipe can be altered to suit your individual taste and what may be available in the larder. For example if you don't have any fresh crabmeat, try chopped defrosted prawns or tinned tuna.

To serve 4
2 ripe avocados
4 oz. crab meat, mix of white and brown
1/2 tsp. chilli pepper, deseeded and finely chopped
2 tbsp. lemon or lime juice
2 tbsp. Hellmann's mayonnaise
4 fl. oz. double cream, whipped
Paprika
Salt & freshly ground black pepper

Halve the avocados, remove the stone and spoon the flesh into a bowl and retain the skins. Mash the avocado flesh and lemon juice, stir in the crabmeat, whipped cream, chilli and mayonnaise and season well. Spoon the mixture back into the avocado skins, sprinkle with a shake or two of paprika and serve with slices of warm buttered toast.

Smoked Salmon with Avocado Cream

You can make the cream for this starter well in advance and store it in the fridge. It is a bit fiddly to lay out on a plate but easy enough to prepare.

To serve 6
24 slices Irish wild smoked salmon (Scottish will do)
2 ripe avocados
1/4 pint double cream
1 tsp. onion, finely grated
1/4 lb. cream cheese
Juice of 1 lemon
3 tsp. salmon eggs
Salt & freshly ground black pepper

Cut the avocados in half, remove the stones and scoop out the flesh. Place in a food processor with the lemon juice, grated onion and the cream cheese and blend. Season well and spoon the mixture into a mixing bowl. Whip the cream until it thickens and fold into the mixture. Cover and store the cream mixture in the fridge until required. Lay four slices of smoked salmon on each plate in a circular fashion, in the shape of a rose head leaving a space in the centre. Carefully spoon in a dollop of the cream to resemble the pollen in the centre of the flower and half a teaspoon of the salmon eggs in the centre of the cream. Serve as a starter with a few slices of brown bread and butter.

Scallop and Artichoke Salad

I love the flavour and texture this combination produces. The soft succulent fish and earthy root marry extremely well together and make a most delicious, simple and rather different salad. As a variation, you could use sweet potato instead of artichoke.

To serve 4
8 large fresh scallops
8 Jerusalem artichokes
Selection of mixed salad leaves
2 tbsp. olive oil
1 tbsp. walnut oil
Juice of half a lemon
Salt and freshly ground pepper

Wash and clean the scallops removing the corals and any sand. Pat dry and slice them into 1/4 inch discs and set aside. Trim the corals and poach them in a little salted water for a minute or two, drain and set aside but save the cooking water. Peel the artichokes and cut them into drum shapes the same width as the scallops, then slice them into 1/4 inch discs. Poach the discs in the same water the corals were cooked in for a minute or two, until they are part cooked but still firm. Drain and set aside. Heat a tablespoon of olive oil in a frying pan until it begins to smoke and flash fry the scallop discs, on one side only, for a few seconds, until they turn golden. Lay the slices on kitchen paper, with the uncooked side down and sprinkle with lemon juice. Prick the corals and in the same oil, flash fry them for a second or two and set aside to drain. Add the artichoke discs to the hot oil for a few seconds and remove, lay white side down on kitchen paper to dry. To assemble the salad, place the leaves in a large bowl. Prepare a vinaigrette of the walnut and olive oil and the rest of the lemon juice, salt and pepper and dress the salad with three-quarters of it. Place a small pile of leaves in the centre of each plate and surround the leaves with a circle of overlapping and alternating discs of scallop and artichoke, fried side up. Scatter the fried corals over the salad leaves with the remaining vinaigrette and serve immediately.

Anchovy Dip (Bagna Cauda)

This is a hearty Italian starter rather like a Swiss fondue and should be served warm. The oven proof dish containing the dip could be kept warm over a candle or spirit heater.

To serve 8 - 10
4 x 2oz tins anchovies in oil
10 cloves garlic, finely chopped
3/4 pint double cream
1/2 lb. butter
1 tsp. each ground black pepper & sea salt
Selection of seasonal vegetables, cut into finger-sized lengths, to include green, yellow or red peppers, celery, spring onions, cucumbers and courgettes
2 slices dry bread

Drain the oil from the anchovies and reserve. Pound the fillets together with the garlic. Melt the butter and mix into the fish paste. Add the cream, retained anchovy oil and pepper. Heat gently but do not boil. Set up over a small flame, if possible, to keep warm or serve straight away as a fondue, allowing guests to dip their choice of vegetable or pieces of bread in the dip.

Pickled Mackerel with Potato Salad

The mackerel can be prepared in advance and stored in jars until required.

To serve 4 - 6
4 mackerel, skinned and filleted [check all bones are removed]
3 fl oz white wine vinegar
3 fl oz water
3 fl oz olive oil
Juice of 1 lemon
1 tbsp. fresh dill, chopped
2 tbsp. brown sugar
1 shallot, finely diced
1 small carrot, finely diced
2 tsp. salt

Cut the mackerel fillets in two and then into 1/2 inch strips and place in a bowl. Mix all the other ingredients together and pour over the fish. Cover the bowl with cling-film and store in the fridge overnight or for up to 18 hours. Prepare some warm potato salad. Place a pile of the potato salad on each plate and then spread some of the mackerel mixture on top of each pile.

Taramasalata

This creamy salad should be made with the rather colourless roe of the grey mullet but smoked cod's roe is more commonly used in the West.

To serve 4 -6
3 oz. smoked cod's roe
1 clove garlic, crushed
2 slices, dry white bread, crusts removed
Juice of 1 lemon
1/2 tsp. cayenne pepper
4 fl oz. olive oil

Skin the roes and place them in a food processor together with the garlic and the cayenne pepper. Squeeze the bread dry, add to the roe and blend. Gradually add the lemon juice and olive oil, as the processor continues to blend the mixture into a smooth cream. Serve in a small bowl with thin slices of toast.

Smoked Salmon Blinis

A small portion would be perfect as a starter or a larger one as a light lunch or snack. I use pre-cooked mashed potato in the blinis mix as it makes a more substantial base for the smoked salmon.

To serve 4
For the blinis
2 oz pre-cooked mashed potato
3 oz self-raising flour
5 fl oz milk
1 egg
Vegetable oil for cooking
1/2 tsp. salt
For the topping
1/2 lb. freshly sliced smoked salmon (preferably wild Irish salmon)
1/2 onion, very finely diced
Greek yoghurt
1 small jar salmon eggs
Paprika
1 lemon, quartered

Heat the mashed potato and a little of the milk in a pan on low heat. Gradually add the rest of the milk to form a paste. Sift the flour and salt into a bowl, beat in the egg and add the potato mixture bit by bit, stirring constantly, to form a creamy batter. Heat some oil in a heavy-based frying pan and spoon in a few rounds of batter, about 2 inches in diameter. When they begin to bubble and rise up, flip them over and cook the other side. They should be firm to the touch and lightly browned on each side. Stack the cooked blinis on a plate and keep warm.
Divide the blinis equally on four plates, arrange the salmon on top of each pile with a sprinkling of chopped onion, a spoonful of yoghurt and top with a teaspoon of salmon eggs. Dust with a little paprika and serve with a quarter of lemon.

Thai Fish Cakes (Tod Man Pla)

These make a simple and delicious starter for any meal.
The fact that coley can be used ensures the cost is reasonable.

To serve 4 - 6
1 lb. boned and skinned coley fillet
2 tbsp. lime zest
2 beaten eggs
1 shallot, finely chopped
2 garlic cloves, grated
1/2 tsp. salt
2 tbsp. Thai fish sauce
1 tsp. sugar
2 tbsp. chopped fresh coriander or broadleaf parsley
Oil for deep-frying
Dipping sauce
3 tbsp. fish sauce
2 tbsp. sugar
1 small chilli, deseeded and finely sliced
4 fl oz rice vinegar
3 shallots, finely sliced
Juice of 1 lemon

Heat the sauce ingredients until the sugar has dissolved and pour into a small bowl. Leave to stand for at least half an hour. Cut the fish into small pieces about 1 inch square, add all the other ingredients and blend to a paste. Check the seasoning. With lightly floured hands, form the mixture into small flat cakes about 2 inches in diameter and about 1/2 inch thick and leave to stand. Heat the oil in a deep pan and when it begins to smoke, add a few of the fish cakes and deep-fry them for about three minutes. Do not try to fry all the cakes in one go. Drain the cakes on a piece of kitchen paper and when all are cooked, serve with the dipping sauce as a starter.

Salmon Carpaccio

Purchase a piece of filleted salmon, cut from the thick end of the
fish with the skin on. In order to be able to carve very thin slices
for this dish, leave it in the freezer for half an hour or so until it
firms up and carve the slices with a very sharp knife.

To serve 4 - 6
2 lb. salmon, filleted
1 cucumber
1 tbsp. lemon juice
3 tbsp. sesame oil
1 tsp. honey
Salt & freshly ground black pepper

Whisk the lemon juice, oil, honey and some salt and pepper to make a dressing. Skin the cucumber and using a potato peeler, peel off a series of very thin strips of cucumber and leave in the dressing for one or two minutes. Slice the fish as though you were slicing smoked salmon and arrange on individual plates. Scatter a few strips of the dressed cucumber on top and drizzle the rest of the dressing over the fish. Serve immediately with a slice or two of buttered bread.

Flambéed Garlic Prawns

This is a simple starter best produced at a small supper party.
Some people lightly boil the prawns before frying them as it
makes shelling them a bit easier.

To serve 6
2 lb. uncooked prawns
1/2 tbsp. ginger, finely grated
1 tbsp. vegetable oil
3 cloves garlic, finely chopped
1 red chilli pepper, deseeded and very finely chopped
2 oz. butter
4 tbsp. Scotch whisky
Thai fish sauce
Handful of salad leaves to decorate each plate

Shell the prawns and set them aside in a bowl with a dash of Thai fish sauce and the grated ginger. Heat the butter and oil in a thick-bottomed frying pan or wok on high heat and fry the garlic for a moment or two but without letting it burn. Add the prawns, fish sauce, chilli and ginger and stir-fry until the prawns change colour and are cooked through. Pour in the whisky and light with a match. When the flames have died down add a dash more Thai fish sauce and a turn or two of freshly ground black pepper. Serve immediately on a bed of salad leaves with some slices of bread and butter.

Smoked Fish Ravioli

Making the pasta dough is easy enough and if you have a pasta machine rolling out the sheets of pasta is a doddle. You can experiment with the filling as much as you like and there are no hard and fast rules. We tend to like to use a blend of smoked and fresh fish because it tastes exciting.

To serve 6 - 8 as a starter
For the pasta
18 oz. plain flour
5 eggs plus an extra yolk
1 tbsp. olive oil
Sea salt
For the filling
8 oz. each of smoked salmon, coley and smoked haddock
5 egg whites
5 oz. ricotta cheese
Bunch of fresh dill
1 tbsp. clotted cream, [optional]
Sea salt & freshly ground black pepper
For the sauce
1 onion, finely chopped
6 cloves garlic, finely chopped
1/2 pint fish stock
2 tbsp. double cream
Sea salt & freshly ground black pepper

Sieve the flour and salt into a mixing bowl, add the eggs and mix well to form a dough. Add the olive oil and continue to knead the dough for 10 minutes or so. Cover the dough with a damp towel and leave aside to rest for 30 minutes. Using a pasta machine pass some of the dough through the machine at ever increasing numbers until you have a very thin sheet. Lay the sheet on a flat floured surface and paint with egg wash or water. Continue to roll sheets of very thin dough until all the dough has been put through the machine.
For the filling, ensure all bones, skin and fins are removed from the fish and place in a food processor with the cheese, egg whites, dill and clotted cream and season well. Whiz until the fish mixture turns into a smooth paste. At this point it is as well to sample the paste to check the flavour. Add more seasoning if required.
To make the sauce, sweat the onion in some butter in a large pan and add the garlic once the onion becomes translucent. Add the fish stock and bring to the boil. Reduce by one third, strain through a fine sieve, add the cream and stir. Check the seasoning and keep warm.
To assemble, place teaspoons of the filling two inches apart across a sheet of dough. Cover with another sheet and gently press the two sheets together. Cut the two sealed sheets into equal sized squares with a fluted wheel cutter and spread on a floured tray.
Cook the ravioli in a large pan of boiling water until al dente, drain with a slotted spoon and serve immediately with the sauce.

Salmon Fishcakes on Spinach

Rather like lamb cutlets, this is a dish commonly found in West End Clubs, old-fashioned restaurants in Brighton and other seaside resorts, or school canteens. They may appear rather ordinary but, if done properly, they are 'historic' as one food commentator is renowned for saying! They make either a delicious starter or light snack.

To serve 6 as a light snack at lunchtime
1 1/2 lb. salmon fillet, skinned
1 1/2 lb. mashed potato
3 anchovy fillets, mashed to a paste
2 tbsp. tomato ketchup or tomato puree
2 tbsp. Coleman's English mustard
2 tsp. Worcestershire sauce
Flour and butter for frying
2 lb. spinach, washed and cleaned
Salt & freshly ground black pepper

Poach the salmon in fish stock if available, if not, dissolve a chicken stock cube in enough water instead. When the fish has been lightly cooked, remove from the stock and flake. Mix together until smooth the potato, half the flaked salmon, ketchup, mustard and anchovy paste and season well. Gently fold in the rest of the salmon flakes and mould the mixture into as many flat round cakes as required. Place all the cakes in the fridge, covered with cling-film, for at least an hour. Lightly flour the fishcakes and fry them in the butter until they are browned on both sides. Keep the cakes warm whilst you prepare the spinach. Put the spinach in a saucepan with the minimum of water, season and cook for about 3 minutes until the leaves are tender. Drain. Place a portion of spinach in the centre of each plate, place a fishcake on top and serve with homemade tomato ketchup.

Dressed Crab

We have fresh dressed crabs shipped up from Cornwall from time to time as a treat. They are always delicious and even the small ones make quite a filling starter. The name of the best West-Country fishmonger we have found, is listed at the back of the book. They can supply picked white and brown crabmeat all year round.

To serve 6
1lb. white crab meat
3 oz. brown crab meat
1/2 tsp. tomato sauce
1/2 tsp. Worcestershire sauce
1 tsp. English mustard
Squeeze of lemon
1 or 2 leaves gelatine
1 fl oz. olive oil
Salt & freshly ground black pepper

Melt the gelatine in a little water, place the white crab meat in a mixing bowl, add half the melted gelatine, a squeeze of lemon and season well. Blend the brown crabmeat, tomato and Worcestershire sauces, mustard and the rest of the gelatine in a food processor to form a smooth sauce. Add the olive oil, slowly, to make a mayonnaise and check the seasoning. Assemble the dish by spooning the white crab meat into 6 suitably sized ring moulds and spoon some of the brown mayonnaise on top. When ready to serve, gently lift off the ring, decorate with a salad leaf or two and a slice of buttered bread.

Salamangundy
(Salmagundi)

An old English salad recipe probably taken from the Norman French word *salmigondis* - *sal* (salt) and *condir* (to season). It became popular in England in the middle of the eighteenth century. It consisted of a selection of small dishes containing a mix of meats, pickled fish, vegetables and pickles and salads of various kinds. One large tray contained saucers or small bowls with a mix of ingredients chosen carefully to blend well together. The choice was massive and included herring or mackerel, pickled cabbage, salted lemon or lime with a number of raw salad leaves, chopped egg yolks, or even cooked chicken or other game birds. Almost anything goes, which is why I have included it here. The layout is as important as the selection of items chosen.

To serve 4 - 6
Arrange 10 small saucers around a central raised dish on a large silver tray. Decorate the tray with a mix of salad leaves and fill each saucer with a different salad item of your choice from the following: -
Thinly sliced or chopped onions
Thinly sliced cucumber
Diced celery, onions, apples or pears
Shredded lettuce or cabbage
Pickled cabbage
Preserved lemons
Pickled gherkins
Hard-boiled egg whites
Hard-boiled egg yolks
Cold, thinly sliced breast of chicken or other fowl

The centre dish may contain one of the following: -
Pickled herring or mackerel, chopped small
Salted anchovies
Smoked salmon or other fish
Chopped salami or other spiced sausage

Each salad dish should be seasoned with a different flavoured dressing and the tray placed in the centre of the table for guests to help themselves.

Hippophagy (The eating of horse flesh)

Eating horsemeat has been common practice in several countries throughout the world including Japan, India, China, South America and surprisingly, Sweden, Holland and Belgium as well. France, however, the country usually thought of as the horse eating capital of the world, banned the eating of horseflesh until after 1811. No doubt the experience of French soldiers during the Napoleonic wars, many of whom survived largely by eating their horses, had some influence in changing public opinion.

Dog

The eating of dog meat is common practice throughout the Far East. In Polynesia, dogs are slowly roasted in underground ovens. In India and Burma, the animals are stuffed and boiled whole. The Chinese like to cure the meat in salt and then stir fry small pieces. The Vietnamese have a recipe for serving dogmeat steaks with wine and in the Philippines, they serve a dogmeat stew with garlic and vinegar. I am told that even the Swiss had a taste for eating dogmeat carpaccio not so many years ago!

Frogs' Legs

Frogs' legs, when fried in butter, taste remarkably like chicken - the thigh meat rather than bland breast meat. Although there are recipes for preparing frog's legs in many parts of the world, including the Middle East and Spain, we tend to think of France as being the country most commonly associated with eating them. They are delicious, seasoned, floured and fried in butter and garlic with a slice of lemon and some parsley as garnish.

Snails

Snails, terrestrial gastropod molluscs, were among the first animals to be eaten by man. Evidence shows that it was the Romans who first prepared them for cooking. The most commonly eaten today are known as Burgundy or Vineyard snails found in the wild, in reducing numbers, in Burgundy, Savoy and Champagne. With the shortage of wild snails in recent years, imports from Turkey and Algeria have increased to meet the demand. All regions of France have their own name for the snail and their own special way of preparing and cooking them. I am fascinated to discover that in the wild, they are the most violent lovers in the animal kingdom. Although they are hermaphrodites, most snails prefer to be males and when wooing a mate they fire darts covered in mucus at the female parts of their intended partners. They tend to be hopeless shots, however, and can cause serious injury to their partners.

Vicomte de Chateaubriand
Author and Gourmet

The Vicomte de Chateaubriand *was joined for dinner by another legendary gourmand, Anthelme Brillat-Savarin, at a Parisian restaurant. The owner announced he had created a new dish, named after the Vicomte in honour of his latest novel,* La Genie Du Christianisme. *It turned out to be a succulent tenderloin steak encased between two thin slices of cheap steak. The outer steaks were seared until black, then discarded; the tenderloin between them remained juicily rare. Chateaubriand steak had been born!*

"*Gourmandism is an act of judgement, by which we prefer things which have a pleasant taste to those which lack this quality.*"
Jean-Anthelme Brillat-Savarin (1755-1826) Preface to **The Physiology of Taste.**

"*Gourmandise is an impassioned, rational and habitual preference for all objects that flatter the sense of taste.*"
Jean-Anthelme Brillat-Savarin (1755-1826) **The Physiology of Taste.**

"*Tell me what you eat, and I'll tell you what you are.*"
Jean-Anthelme Brillat-Savarin

"*None for me. I appreciate the potato only as a protection against famine; except for that, I know of nothing more eminently tasteless.*"
Jean-Anthelme Brillat-Savarin

Catherine de Medici, Queen of France

Catherine de Medici was born in 1519, the daughter and sole heir of the Florentine ruler, Lorenzo the Magnificent. She was orphaned within a month of her birth and was brought up by nuns in a convent under the control of her uncle, Pope Clement VII. At the tender age of 14 she was sent to France to marry the Duc d'Orleans, who became King Henry II in 1547. The snobbish French considered her little more than the daughter of a minor Italian princeling on her arrival at court, although her dowry included the city state of Florence. When she died in 1589, however, she had seen her husband and three of her sons crowned Kings of France.

She was tiny, less than five foot tall and not particularly attractive but she managed to make the most of herself. She secretly wore a pair of specially designed high-heeled shoes at her wedding which not only made her appear taller but gave her walk a subtle undulation, a gentle seductive sway, the like of which the French had never seen before.

In the early years she lead a very lonely life at court as the King spent most of his time in the arms of his mistress, Diane de Poitiers. As a result Catherine surrounded herself with friends and relations from Florence including a retinue of cooks who brought with them delicious delicacies such as macaroons, sorbets and zabaglione. Apart from pasta, they introduced fruit and vegetables to France including artichokes, melons and broccoli.

Catherine loved her food, an early gourmand who ended her days so portly she found walking a great strain. She entertained in regal style, decorating her table with silver and gold ornaments and a profusion of flowers. She insisted on her guests using forks to eat with at table, not just to take food from the serving platters. The French, used to much rougher dining habits with tankards, wood platters and simple knives, found her use of delicate wine glasses, gold and silver plates and forks a slight on their masculinity. They were slow to accept the use of the fork and the fashion didn't catch on in France until two hundred years after her death.

Her cousin, Marie de Medici, also married into the French royal family. Her contribution to the French culinary scene was the introduction puff pastry. This method of pastry making, using layers of fat in the dough, led to the development of the croissant and the fruit pastries so closely associated with France today.

MEAT BASED STARTERS

Strictly speaking the word pâté on its own in France would be used only when applied to a dish consisting of a pastry shell stuffed with meat or vegetables, cooked and served hot or cold. The English equivalent for the word would likely be 'pie' although in English, a pie describes dishes not nearly as complex and elaborate. In both French and English, meat or fish cooked in a dish and served cold, is known as pâté en terrine, abbreviated to simply terrine in both languages.

Now we have that out of the way we can get down to describing a few easy to prepare, meat based starters and snacks. Although we were quite determined not to include too many chicken dishes, as they tend to be so boring, we have included a few that we think original.

Spiced Chicken Wings

This is the perfect 'Fat boy' snack. They can be eaten any time of the day. Excellent as a starter at a summer barbecue or warm in front of a blazing fire and your favourite television programme. They were made famous in the States as 'The Anchor Bar Buffalo Wings' and the sauce that went with them is available on the internet. I think it is fun to design your own sauce, however, although I give below one I think goes well with the wings.

To serve 4
16 fresh whole chicken wings
For the sauce
4 oz brown sugar
Juice from 2 lemons
1 tbsp. finely grated fresh ginger
2 tbsp. tomato puree [optional]
4 tbsp. soy sauce
1 tsp. English mustard powder
1 tsp. salt
1/2 tsp. black pepper
6 fl oz water
1 tbsp. cornstarch

Remove the tips from the chicken wings and either discard them or freeze them for use in making chicken stock at a later time. With a sharp knife, cut each wing in half through the joint and wash them in running water. Dry the wings on kitchen paper and place them in a single layer in an ovenproof pan. Bake in a hot oven for around 30 minutes, turning once. While the chicken is baking, mix together the sugar, cornstarch, salt and pepper in a saucepan, add the water, lemon juice and soy sauce and simmer, stirring constantly, until the sauce thickens. Brush the sauce onto the wings and continue baking, basting from time to time with the sauce, for a further 30 minutes until the wings are well cooked. Serve hot with lots of paper towels to take care of sticky fingers. We don't want the beer glass slipping through our fingers!

Chicken Satay

These small skewers of chicken with their peanut sauce make a most delicious starter for a Thai curry evening or indeed as a starter for any meal. Thin slices of pork or fillet steak could be used as well.

To serve 4
4 chicken breasts
For the marinade
7 fl oz. soy sauce
2 garlic cloves, crushed
1 tsp. each, finely chopped ginger and chopped coriander
For the sauce
8 oz. peanut butter, the thick crunchy variety
4 fl oz. coconut milk
2 garlic cloves, crushed
2 fl oz. soy sauce
1/4 tsp. cayenne pepper

Mix all the marinade ingredients together in a shallow dish. Chop the chicken breasts into 3/4 inch cubes and cover them with some clingfilm. Hammer the cubes with a meat mallet to flatten slightly and thread them onto wooden skewers up to half way down each skewer. Place the skewers in the marinade and leave in the fridge overnight or longer if possible. Turn the skewers in the marinade from time to time.

Blend the peanut butter, soy sauce, coconut milk, cayenne pepper and garlic into a smooth paste in a food processor. Should the sauce appear too thick for dunking, add a drop or two of water to thin it. When ready to cook, take the skewers from the marinade and either cook them on the barbecue or fry or grill them for no more than 6 minutes. Serve 3 or 4 skewers to each guest with a small dish of sauce each or let them help themselves to the skewers from a central platter.

Tony's Stuffed Chicken Breasts

These poached sausages are an excellent stand-by for last-minute lunches or starters at supper parties. They are not that difficult to prepare and can be kept wrapped in clingfilm in the freezer or the fridge until required. The important thing is to ensure that the stuffing has plenty of flavour, which can be adjusted according to your personal taste and inclination.

To feed 4 as a light supper or as a starter for dinner
1 large chicken
1 large egg
2oz tin anchovy fillets
1 tsp. grated nutmeg
1 onion, chopped
6 garlic cloves, chopped
1 1/2 tsp. curry powder [optional]
1 hot red chilli, chopped
Salt & freshly ground black pepper

Cut off both sides of the chicken breast and remove the skin. Place each side in turn on a long piece of clingfilm, fold the clingfilm over the breast and hammer the meat until it is little more than an 1/4 inch thick. Encourage it to form a square shape. Set aside, still wrapped in clingfilm. Remove the meat from the legs and thighs of the chicken. Discard the skin, cut into pieces and place in a food processor with the chopped onion, anchovy, nutmeg, curry powder, garlic, chilli and egg. Blend to a paste and add plenty of seasoning. Gently peel back the top layer of clingfilm on each beaten breast and place half the stuffing across the centre. Carefully roll the meat into a sausage shape by folding the clingfilm around it. Be careful not to wrap the meat too tightly because it will expand somewhat when cooked. Ensure that the clingfilm at the ends of the sausage are twisted tight so that they remain closed whilst being cooked. Place the sausages in a pan of boiling water and simmer for at least 30 minutes. Check from time to time to ensure that the sausages are turned in the water so they are cooked through. Allow to cool and either store in the fridge until required, or remove the clingfilm and cut into 1/4-inch slices. Serve on a piece of lettuce with a sweet and sour or onion marmalade.

Beef Marrow Toast

Your butcher should be able to let you have a few marrow bones but make sure they do not include the knuckle ends as they don't contain any marrow. This reminds me so much of dunking slices of bread in the juices left behind when the roast beef has been moved to the carving board. Oh! Heaven!

To serve 4
4 marrow bones cut to 3 or 4 inch lengths
4 slices brown bread, crusts removed
Olive oil
Sea salt

Roast the marrow bones in the oven until the marrow becomes loose but doesn't melt. Fry the slices of bread in some olive oil until crisp and brown. Hold the bones with an oven glove, spoon out the marrow and spread it onto each piece of fried bread. Sprinkle with a little sea salt and eat straight away. Fantastic!

Braised Kidneys in Madeira Sauce

This simple and flexible dish is easy to prepare and can be served for 'brunch' or as a starter for lunch or supper.

To serve 6
12 lamb's kidneys
1 large onion, finely sliced
8 oz. small button mushrooms, halved
6 fl.oz. Madeira (if Madeira is not available, try sweet sherry)
4 fl.oz. beef stock
Butter and olive oil for frying
Plain, seasoned flour for dusting
6 slices of toast, crusts removed
Salt & freshly ground black pepper

Remove any fat or skin from the kidneys and slice them in half. With scissors or a very sharp knife, cut out the white cores, wash and pat dry with kitchen paper. Cut the kidneys into chunks and dust them with seasoned flour. Sweat the sliced onion in butter and olive oil until translucent, add the kidneys and mushrooms and stir fry for a few minutes to seal the kidneys and soften the mushrooms. Add the Madeira and stock, bring to the boil and simmer for 10 minutes or so until the kidneys are cooked through and the sauce has thickened. Adjust the seasoning and serve on the toast.

Chicken Liver Mousseline

Individual mousselines make an easy starter and
if served cold, can be prepared well in advance.
The sauce needs to be concentrated and very rich
to improve the rather bland flavour of the liver.

To serve 8
1/2 lb. chicken livers
Milk for soaking
1/2 pint full cream milk
1/2 pint double cream
3 eggs
3 egg yolks
1/4 pint chicken stock
1 tbsp. tomato concentrate
6 tbsp. ruby port
3 oz. butter, chilled
1 small onion, finely chopped
1 tomato, skinned, deseeded and chopped
Salt & freshly ground black pepper

Soak the chicken livers in milk for half an hour or so to remove any trace of blood, pat dry and remove the gall. Chop roughly and place in a blender with the milk, cream and eggs and puree until smooth. Season well and blend for a second or two more. Force the mixture through a fine sieve and store in the fridge to cool. Butter eight small ramekins and fill with the mixture. Cover with a sheet of greaseproof paper and place the ramekins in an oven-roasting pan half filled with hot water and cook in a medium oven for 20 minutes, until firm. Allow the ramekins to cool, covered, until you are ready to serve the dish.

To make the sauce, melt half the butter in a saucepan and sweat the onion until transparent. Add the port and chicken stock, bring to the boil and reduce by half. Add the tomato concentrate and simmer for a few moments more. Liquidise the sauce in a blender, dice the remaining chilled butter and whisk into the sauce. When you are ready to serve, carefully shake out the mousselines onto the centre of each plate, drizzle the sauce around and sprinkle the top of each with the chopped tomato.

Confit of Pork with Scallops and Noodle Salad

This recipe is contributed courtesy of one of Australia's most exciting chefs, Peter Gilmore of " Quay ", the award-winning restaurant in the terminal building in Sydney Harbour. I have been forced to adjust some of the ingredients as they are not readily available here, but I believe the result is quite superb.

This recipe was described as an entree, however if the meat portion per person is increased it makes a great 'Fat boy' lunch.

To serve 4
1 lb. pork belly trimmed and boned
8 large fresh scallops [corals removed]
2 oz dried fine white Japanese wheat noodles or, alternatively, fine rice noodles
1 oz black fungi mushrooms [Sometimes called black & white Fungus,1 oz after soaking]
1 oz shiitake mushrooms [if no fresh are available, 1 oz after soaking]
1 oz salted jelly fish [if available]
10 sprigs fresh baby coriander
1 tsp. sesame seeds
1 tbsp. grape-seed oil
1 tbsp. mirrin or sweetened Chinese rice wine
1 tbsp. light soy sauce [salt reduced]
1 pint of chicken stock

Slowly confit the pork belly in olive oil for up to 7 hours in the bottom of the Aga or in an oven at 120c. When cooked, cool and press the meat between two clingfilm lined trays with a weight on top. Leave in the fridge for a minimum of 4 hours. Boil the chicken stock and reduce to about 3 tablespoons, add half the soy sauce and mirrin and continue to reduce further to form a thick glaze to coat the pork. Set aside and keep warm. Soak the dried mushrooms according to the instructions on the packages, slice them finely and sauté in a little butter. Set aside to cool. Cook the noodles in boiling water for one minute or so, rinse under cold water to avoid them sticking and set aside to cool. Add the remaining mirrin and soy sauce to the grapeseed-oil and whisk to form a dressing for the noodle salad. To assemble, cut the pork into eight equal rectangular pieces. Seal the pork pieces on each side in a very hot pan then roast, skin side down, in the oven for five minutes until the skin is crisp. Mix the noodles, mushrooms, jellyfish, sesame seeds and coriander together with the dressing. Place equal quantities of the noodles between two pieces of pork on each plate and coat the pork with the glaze. Sear the scallops for a second or two and place two on top of each pile of noodles. Serve immediately.

Slow-Cooked Pork Belly and Lentils

This recipe is, of course, meant to be a main course but if you cut back just a bit on the lentils and cut the pork belly a little thinner I think it passes for a superb 'Fat Boy' starter or snack. The other great advantage of slow-cooking pork is that you can leave it in a slow oven all day for supper at night.

To serve 4 or 6
3lbs. pork belly
6 cloves garlic
2 tbsp. fennel seeds
1 tsp. black pepper
Juice 1 lemon
2 dried chillis
3 tbsp. puy lentils per person
Chicken stock
2 carrots, very finely diced
1 onion, very finely diced
Olive oil & balsamic vinegar
Large handful of parsley, finely chopped
Salt and freshly ground black pepper

Remove any rib bones from the belly of pork, dry the rind and rub with salt. Place the pork, rind side up, under the grill until it starts to crackle then remove and allow it to cool. Grind three cloves of garlic, the fennel seeds, chillis, lemon juice and pepper together to make a paste and rub it into the pork on all sides except the rind. Place the meat on a rack over hot water in a roasting tin and place it in the bottom of the Aga or in a slow oven and forget about it overnight or for at least nine or ten hours, until the meat is so tender it could be cut with a fork.
Rinse the lentils in cold running water, drain, add the remaining garlic cloves and pour over sufficient chicken stock to cover and bring to the boil. Simmer for fifteen minutes or until the lentils are tender. Drain and set aside. Fry the finely diced carrot and onion until they begin to sweat, add the lentils and season well, stir in two or three tablespoons of the vinegar and allow it to reduce slightly. Check the seasoning, add more salt if necessary, a tablespoon or two of olive oil and the chopped parsley.
Place the pork back under the grill to dry out the rind, then place it rind side down on a chopping board and cut it into sufficient pieces, about an inch thick. Spoon the lentils onto the plates and put a piece of pork on top. Real 'Fat boy' food!

Black Pudding with Foie Gras

*We first tried this combination in a restaurant in London many years ago and thought it quite superb. Getting hold of foie gras may prove a bit of a problem, however, but the dish is easy to prepare.
This is pure 'Fat boy' food!*

To feed 4 as a starter
*4 discs of black pudding about 2 inches across and 1/2 inch thick
4 slices foie gras [not the pate] about 1/2 inch thick, cut to fit on the black pudding
4 eggs
Butter
Salt & pepper*

Poach the eggs and keep them warm in a bowl of warm water. Gently fry the black pudding discs on both sides and set each in the centre of a plate. Fry the foie gras very rapidly on very hot heat on both sides and place on the black puddings. Remove the eggs with a slotted spoon and place on top of the foie gras on each plate and serve seasoned with the salt and pepper. Heaven!

Black Pudding Fritters

These delicious deep-fried parcels can be served as a snack, starter or even as a light main course served with chips or mashed potatoes and pickled onions.

To serve 4
*8 oz. black pudding, peeled and chopped into 1 inch cubes
8 oz. self-raising flour
Vegetable oil for deep frying
8 fl oz. lager
Salt & freshly ground black pepper*

Heat the oil in a deep pan. Make a batter by sifting the flour into a bowl and whisk in sufficient lager to make a fairly thick batter. Dust the black pudding cubes with some flour and, with a fork, dip them in the batter, ensuring they are completely covered. Carefully drop the cubes into the oil in batches and cook for around three to five minutes until the outsides are crisp and golden. Remove with a slotted spoon and leave on kitchen paper to drain off any surplus oil, then sprinkle with salt and pepper. Divide into four equal portions and serve.

Liver Dumplings (Lewerknepfles)

These dumplings from Germany are considered better than the ones found in Alsace and are perfect as a starter served with finely sliced onion fried in butter.

To serve 8 as a starter
8oz pork or beef liver, finely chopped
2oz pork fat, finely chopped
1 onion, finely chopped
1/2 oz butter
2oz plain white flour
2 eggs
2 cloves garlic, crushed
1/2 tsp. each nutmeg and allspice
3oz breadcrumbs
1 tbsp. parsley, chopped
Salt and freshly ground black pepper

Fry the chopped onion in butter until soft and brown. Mix together in a bowl, the liver and pork fat with the fried onion, garlic, breadcrumbs, eggs, flour, spices and salt and pepper. Bring a pot of salted water to the boil and reduce the heat. Using two teaspoons dipped in the hot water, shape the mixture into oval shapes and slide them carefully into the simmering water. Poach the dumplings slowly for about eight or nine minutes. Do not allow the water to boil or the dumplings will break up. Remove with a slotted spoon and keep them warm in a serving dish. Serve with finely sliced onion rings, fried in butter until brown, scattered over the top.

Devon Potted Meat

Meat has been potted in England, as a means of preserving it, since the Middle Ages and this coarse paste is ideal for a light supper starter.

To serve 6
8 oz. pork sausage meat
8 oz. chicken livers
4 oz. bacon, rind removed
1 onion, roughly chopped
2 cloves garlic, crushed
1 tbsp. double cream
1 tbsp. brandy
Pinch each of dried thyme and marjoram
Salt & freshly ground black pepper

Place the onion, garlic, sausage meat and chicken livers in a mixer and blend to a rough paste. Stir in the brandy, herbs and cream and season well. Line a 1 pint ovenproof dish or a 1 lb. loaf tin, with the bacon and spoon the mixture into the tin. Cover with tin foil and bake in a medium oven for 2 hours. Remove from the oven and allow to cool with a weight on top for at least 8 hours in a cool place. To serve, remove the weight and turn out onto a serving plate or cut into individual portions. Serve with plenty of toast.

Pork Terrine

I have chosen to include this very basic terrine because it is simple to make and yet extremely tasty. There are plenty of ways in which this recipe can be personalised.

To serve 6 - 8
1/2 lb. sausage meat
1/2 lb. minced pork
1/2 lb. lamb's liver
1/2 lb. veal (or pork)
2 eggs, hard boiled and finely chopped
6 rashers streaky bacon
1 onion, peeled and roughly chopped
2 cloves garlic, peeled and chopped
1 wine glass, port
1/2 tsp. dried thyme
1/2 tsp. parsley, finely chopped
4 or 5 bay leaves
Salt & freshly ground black pepper

Line the sides and bottom of a small terrine or lidded dish with the bacon rashers. Mince the liver, onion and garlic in a food processor until smooth, add the sausage meat and continue to mince until well blended. Pour in the port, add the herbs, season well and stir in the chopped egg. Place a layer of this mixture in the bottom of the terrine. Cut the veal into thin strips and place some strips on top of the mixture. Place more of the mixture over the strips and then alternate layers of meat and mixture until finally you end with a layer of the mixture. Press the bay leaves onto the top and cover the terrine with a lid. Stand the terrine in an oven tin, fill with boiling water half way up the terrine and cook in a hot oven for 1 1/2 hours. Remove the lid, cover the top of the pate with foil and place a heavy weight on top. Leave for at least 24 hours to cool and for the terrine to mature. Serve with thick slices of wholemeal bread and some onion marmalade.

Chopped Liver

Liver chopped to a paste is one of the best-known Jewish foods apart from gefilte fish, which is also included in this book. It is simple to make, provides an excellent starter for almost any meal and is not expensive. I like it because, when it's available in the fridge, I can usually get away with a quick dip before anyone notices. The ingredients never change but the quantities are up to you and your conscience. I like to add a drop or two of brandy but Madeira goes well with liver too, - things I doubt would be included in a Jewish household recipe.

To serve 4
9 oz. chicken livers
1 onion, peeled and finely chopped
2 hard-boiled eggs
2 tbsp. olive or other milder flavoured oil
Brandy or Madeira
Salt & freshly ground black pepper

Fry the onion in oil until it turns soft and golden. Rinse the livers in milk and remove any sign of blood or sinew. Fry the livers briefly with the onion until they start to change colour. Allow them to cool. Peel the hard-boiled eggs and chop finely in a food processor and place in a serving bowl. Chop the onion and liver briefly in the food processor but leave the mixture quite coarse. Remove a tablespoon of chopped egg from the bowl for garnish, and fold in the onion and liver. Season with salt and pepper, a drop or two of brandy and mix well. Smooth the surface, sprinkle with the reserved chopped egg and serve with slices of warm, freshly baked bread.

The Tomato

The tomato comes originally from the western coast of South America, in present-day Peru, where eight species of the genus still grow wild in the foothills of the Andes. The tomato, from the Aztec word 'tomatl', is believed to have been first cultivated around 3000 years ago.

The 16th century conquistadors are thought to have introduced them to Spain, where their popularity spread quickly to Portugal, Italy and throughout Europe.

These first cultivars were small, cherry-like yellow fruits which became known as 'manzanas' (apples) in Spain, 'pomi d'oro' (golden apples) by the Italians and 'pomme d'amour' (love apple) by the French.

A German botanist was responsible for naming the tomato - Lycopersicon esculentum, meaning 'edible wolf peach'. He mistakenly took the tomato for the wolfpeach, referred to by Galen in his third century writings, a poison in a palatable package which was used to destroy wolves.

The earliest mention of the tomato in European literature appeared in a document written in 1544 by Pietro Andrea Mattioli, an Italian physician and botanist. His review, however, was bad press for the tomato because he linked it to other members of the Solanaceae family, notably the poisonous plant, deadly nightshade (Atropus belladonna).

The English form 'tomate' first appeared in print in 1595, and was later modified to 'tomato'.

Although tomatoes were slow to catch on in England as edible fruits or vegetables, a tomato recipe did appear in 'The Art of Cookery' by Hannah Glass in 1758.

Still, it was not until the 1830s that the tomato was much more than a curiosity in America. They were slow to take to the tomato and in fact it wasn't until Colonel Robert Gibbon Johnson stood on the steps of the courthouse in Salem, Massachusetts with a basket of tomatoes, offering to eat them all to prove they were not poisonous, that Americans began to accept them as edible.

They are now considered healthy because they contain the antioxidant lycopene, noted for its ability to reduce the risk of prostate cancer in men. They also contain vitamin C and carotenoids, beta carotene being one of the most familiar, which are antioxidants. These offer protection from free radicals that cause premature ageing, cancer, heart disease, and cataracts. Loaded with antioxidants and high in potassium, tomatoes are one of the healthiest "vegetables" around.

If you happen to be unfortunate enough to get sprayed by a skunk, tomato juice will neutralize butyl mercaptan, the prime ingredient in the animal's defensive spray.

And finally, the world record for the largest tomato is held by Charles Roberts of Great Britain, who in 1974 harvested a whopper weighing four pounds, four ounces.

"Garlick maketh a man wynke, drynke, and stynke."
--Thomas Nashe, 16th century poet.

Garlic, Allium sativum, *is a bulbous plant about the size of a child's fist belonging to the lily family which includes onions, leeks, chives, and shallots. The name derives from the Celtic word* allium, *meaning "hot or burning," and the Latin* sativum *meaning "cultivated." Our word 'garlic' is from the Anglo-Saxon* garleac, *a combination of* gar *meaning spear and* lac *meaning leek.*

Once a wild herb, today's garlic is cultivated throughout the world, though some still grows wild in the Ukraine and Afghanistan. It probably originated in central Asia and has been known for hundreds of years for its curative properties. It is thought likely that the Crusaders introduced it to Western Europe where it was considered something of a panacea for a host of ailments from digestive discomforts and intestinal infections to high blood pressure, senility, and impotence.

Egyptian Archeologists discovered clay sculptures of garlic bulbs dating back to 3700 BC and early Greek military leaders employed garlic to embolden their warriors at the outset of battle. [Perhaps, breathing on their enemies helped to ensure victory]. Early Greek Olympic athletes are said to have chewed on garlic to boost their performance.

The Greek aristocracy, however, firmly rejected garlic and found its smell repugnant. Anyone smelling of garlic was considered vulgar and was prevented from entering the temples. Aristotle, on the other hand, listed garlic among the foods he considered aphrodisiacs. Like the Greeks, the early Roman nobility did not eat garlic but considered the herb worthy only of being fed to their labourers and slaves, to give them strength and vigour.

The ancient Hebrews credited garlic for its ability to satiate hunger, improve blood circulation, kill parasites, cure jealousy, keep the body warm, and as an aphrodisiac. The Talmud, amusingly, encourages eating garlic on Friday because making love on the Sabbath is considered a good thing to do. No doubt why garlic extract has even been hailed as a "veggie viagra."

British army doctors created a juice of raw garlic diluted with water and applied it directly to wounds to control infections during World War I. The garlic juice was so successful in treating infection that Russian army physicians employed the same technique in World War II.

Recent research reveals garlic is quite effective in keeping mosquitoes at bay and it also works well to discourage aphids and white flies in the garden.

During the Middle Ages, English cookery was awash with recipes that employed garlic in sauces for meats, poultry, and even salads. Richard II dined on an elaborate salad made with garlic, parsley, sage, onions, leeks, borage, mint, greens, fennel, watercress, rue, rosemary and purslane.

Unusual in the world of horticulture, garlic, is considered sterile and does not grow from a seed but is grown from the individual cloves that cluster together to form a bulb or head.

.

"Eat leeks in March and garlic in May,
Then the rest of the year, your doctor can play."

Coriander

Coriandrum sativum, *an aromatic, umbelliferous plant named after the Greek, koros, meaning bug, is indigenous to Southern Europe. The ancient Greeks found the smell of the young seed pods or fruit unpleasant whereas in Peru they are so fond of the herb that it is used to flavour almost all their dishes. The seed pods, grown in clusters of tiny round balls, lose their disagreeable scent after drying. It has been used in one form or another for over 7,000 years and is now one of the most common herbs in the world although ironically, in France its use tends to be limited to the manufacture of liqueurs such as Chartreuse. In the late 1990's it was the 'in' herb and the leaves were used to decorate dishes as much as parsley used to be. It was introduced to South America by the Spanish conquistadors and is still known there by its Spanish name, cilantro. The Romans used it for preserving meat, the Jews for flavouring bread. In India it is an important ingredient in curry powder and in Morocco and other parts of North Africa it is used extensively in a marinade called chermoula and to flavour the ubiquitous tagine. It was introduced to Britain by the Romans and these days it is grown commercially in Essex. Apart from the use here of its seeds and leaves as a culinary herb, distillers use the seeds to make gin and vets use them to make a drug for horses and cattle.*

EGG, VEGETABLE and OTHER STARTERS

Eggs are a perfectly balanced food, fairly low in calories. The yolk represents 30% of the weight of an egg and the albumen, or white of the egg, around 60%. Eggshells are porous and fresh eggs lose a tiny portion of their weight each day through evaporation. Fresh eggs, therefore, are heavy and as a result a really fresh egg would immediately sink to the bottom of a bowl containing salted water. I only mention this earth-shattering piece of information as this is the best way of checking how fresh an egg really is. Eggs are cheap, nutritious and probably the most versatile ingredient in cooking. Fresh eggs can be frozen if they are cracked into a bowl, whipped and poured into a suitable container. It is not wise, however, to store egg yolks or the white of eggs in a fridge for longer than a couple of days. In fact, some experts claim storing uncooked egg whites for longer than a few hours could be dangerous.

Eggs became a part of the human diet from earliest days and were often involved in religious rites or traditions. The Romans insisted on crushing the empty shells on their platters to ensure that evil spirits had nowhere to hide. To this day the empty shells of boiled eggs are holed by the superstitious " to prevent a sailor drowning."

As for vegetables, John Davenport wrote in his 1859 essay, *Aphrodisiacs & Anti-Aphrodisiacs* about the various vegetables which might help *'for strengthening the genital apparatus, and exciting it to action.'* The Romans too, appear to have embraced love potions in a serious way, prompting Martial's verse:

If envious age relax the nuptial knot
Thy food be mushrooms, and thy feast shallot

Different parts of vegetables could be included as potential ingredients for starters, the fruit for example such as courgettes, aubergines, peppers and tomatoes; the seed such as peas, beans and lentils; the leaf such as lettuce, spinach and cabbage; the bulb such as onions, fennel and shallots and roots. There is a general misconception about 'roots'. Not all roots are truly roots; some such as potatoes, Jerusalem artichokes, sweet potatoes and yams, are tubers. Others such as celeriac, turnips and swedes are swollen stem bases and might correctly be described as brassicas. Mushrooms and other fungi are also usually regarded as vegetables. However, when experimenting with various roots as potential ingredients for starters we came up with one or two irresistible ideas.

Leeks with Egg Vinaigrette

This salad can be served as a starter or to accompany a barbecue. Choose young leeks, no thicker than a fat stem of asparagus. The salad can also be made with broccoli.

To serve 6
10 thin leeks or 6 thicker ones, trimmed, washed and cleaned of grit
2 hard-boiled eggs
2 tbsp. white wine vinegar
1 tsp. English mustard powder
2 garlic cloves, peeled and crushed
4 - 5 tbsp. extra virgin olive oil
Chopped parsley
Salt & freshly ground black pepper

Cut the leeks into 3 inch lengths and boil in salted water until tender, about 5 minutes. Remove with a slotted and spoon and refresh in cold water. Drain in a colander and dry on kitchen paper. Pour the vinegar and olive oil into a mixing bowl and whisk in the mustard powder. Mash the crushed garlic and some salt into a paste and whisk into the vinaigrette until it begins to thicken, taste and adjust the seasoning. Lay the leeks out in a single layer on an oval serving dish, dice the eggs and sprinkle over the leeks. Give the vinaigrette a final whisk and pour it over. Allow to stand for 2 or 3 hours to marinate and serve decorated with a little chopped parsley.

Baked Artichoke and Horseradish Cream

These tasty little treats make a welcome change from other
more complicated starters and are extremely easy to prepare.

To serve 6
6 round Jerusalem artichokes about the size of golf balls, well scrubbed
3 oz. butter
1 slice, smoked bacon
6 tbsp. double cream
2 tbsp. creamed horseradish
3 tsp. salmon eggs
Salt and freshly ground black pepper

Place the artichokes in an oven proof dish, cover with butter and the smoked bacon, season well and bake in a hot oven for 30-40 minutes until cooked. Allow to cool and cut of the top of each root to open them up. Whip the cream and horseradish together to thicken and place a spoonful on each plate and top with the prepared artichoke. Spoon a portion of the salmon eggs onto each and serve.

Pasta with Sea Urchin
(Tagliatelle al Ricci di Mare)

I saw this dish described in a newspaper article recently and
decided to try it out. It is easy to prepare and makes a change
from the usual tomato based sauces so popular with lazy cooks.
Getting hold of sea urchin roe might be a problem but it can be
bought from specialist Italian suppliers in tins over the internet. I
have given the contact details of one such company at the back
of the book. This dish can be served as a starter or light lunch
or supper.

To serve 4
3oz. dry tagliatelle
2 garlic cloves
1 handful chopped parsley
4 tbsp. virgin olive oil
1 tbsp. sea urchin roe
Freshly ground black pepper

Cook the tagliatelle al dente in lots of salted water. Drain the sea urchin and whisk with a tablespoon of olive oil. Crush the garlic cloves in oil and fry lightly for a minute or two. Drain the tagliatelle and fry gently for a minute or two with the garlic. Remove from the heat and toss with the sea urchin sauce and sprinkle with the chopped parsley.

Cheese Fondue

I think a fondue makes a wonderful light supper for a group of four around the kitchen table next to the Aga when it's miserably cold outside. It pays to follow the traditional Swiss recipe and keep it simple. Some cheeses mix well together, others do not. One or two important things to watch out for - avoid boiling the cheese, always use stale or four-day old bread if possible and never drink cold water with a cheese fondue, it will turn the cheese into a solid indigestible lump in your stomach.

To serve 4
1 lb. Gruyere
1/2 lb. Emmental
1 pint dry white wine [Riesling or Gewürztraminer]
1 small wine glass kirsch
Pinch of nutmeg
West Country alternative ingredients
1 lb. strong farmhouse Cheddar
1/2 lb. Emmanthal
1 pint Devonshire farm cider
1 small wine glass Somerset apple brandy
Pinch of nutmeg

Grate the cheeses into a bowl, add a pinch of nutmeg and a glass or two of the wine or cider and allow the mixture to stand for an hour, until you are ready to prepare the fondue. Bring the rest of the wine to the boil in a fondue pan, reduce the heat and add the cheese mixture, stirring constantly in a figure of eight motion until the mixture is well blended. Add the glass of kirsch and continue to stir until you are satisfied with the texture. If the mixture is too thin, add a little cornflour dissolved in some kirsch and turn up the heat slightly. If too thick, add a little more wine. Serve with cubes of lightly toasted dried bread and a bottle or two of Riesling or Gewürztraminer. Try dipping the bread briefly in a glass of kirsch before dunking it in the cheese and ensure, that when dunking, you stir the fondue in a figure of eight motion to avoid the cheese sticking to the bottom of the pan or separating on the top.

Tartiflette

This is a deliciously extravagant 'Fat Boy' starter, a sort of *abat-faim*, which could make an excellent snack or light lunch. Like so many recipes it can be easily personalised. We like to add a glass of white wine to the double cream but you could use a dash of mustard and some grated nutmeg with crème fraiche instead. Should you be unable to find any Reblochon cheese, try Gruyere or Epoisses

To serve 4
1 1/2 lbs. potatoes, peeled and par-boiled
1 large onion, peeled and thinly sliced
7 oz. pancetta or smoked bacon cut into lardons
1 Reblochon cheese, sliced into two discs
1 pint, double cream or crème fraiche
1 glass, dry white wine
Butter and olive oil for frying
Salt & freshly ground black pepper

Fry the onion and pancetta until the onion begins to colour. Remove with a slotted spoon and drain on kitchen paper. Cut the potatoes into 1/2 inch dice and fry them in the remaining butter until they begin to crisp. Place the onion, pancetta and potato mixture in a low sided casserole dish, pour the cream and wine over the mixture, season and mix well. Place the discs of Reblochon on top, with the skin sides uppermost and cook, covered with tinfoil, in a hot oven for about an hour. Remove the tinfoil and return the casserole to the oven for a further 10 or 15 minutes to brown the top. Allow the dish to stand, covered, for half an hour before serving. Delicious with a glass or two of a good strong red wine. As an alternative, allow the dish to cool, store it in the fridge and serve cold cut in slices like a quiche.

Chakchouka

A very simple North African dish which could either be served as a starter at dinner or as a light lunch or supper. It could have been called 'three into one' I suppose. This is not truly 'Fat boy' food, but I have included it because if I get peckish mid-morning, it makes a delicious snack before lunch!

To serve 4 as a starter
3 large tomatoes, skinned, deseeded and chopped
3 green peppers, deseeded and chopped
3 medium sized aubergine cut into discs
3 onions, peeled and sliced
3 courgettes, chopped
3 garlic cloves, peeled and crushed
4 eggs
Salt & pepper
2 fresh green chillies, deseeded and finely sliced
Olive oil

Sprinkle the aubergine discs on both sides with salt and leave for a while to sweat, then drain and dry them on kitchen paper. Put the chopped tomato into a large heavy ovenproof dish or casserole and leave them to sweat in their own juice for a minute or two. Add a good 4 or 5 tbsp. of olive oil, the other vegetables, garlic and chillies and season well. Simmer, covered, on a hot plate for 10 minutes or until all the ingredients are cooked. Remove the lid and make four hollows in the mixture and break an egg into each. Place, uncovered, in a hot oven for 3 or 4 minutes and serve in the casserole as soon as the eggs have set, with a grind or two of black pepper.

Stuffed Aubergine Rolls

To serve 6
2 large aubergine
1 red chilli, deseeded and finely chopped
10 oz. feta cheese
1 handful fresh mint, finely chopped
Juice of one lemon
Salt & freshly ground black pepper

Slice the aubergine lengthways into about eight slices, discarding the outside slices. Brush both sides of the slices with olive oil and cook on a griddle pan until browned on each side. Place the chopped chilli, mint and lemon juice in a bowl, season well and mix gently. Crumble the feta cheese into the bowl and stir. Place a spoonful of the mixture on each slice of aubergine, roll up and secure with a tooth pick or cocktail stick. Serve warm with a drizzle of olive oil and a quarter of lemon.

Fried Egg & Bacon Toasties

There is nothing simpler than egg and fried bread, it's good for a starter or simple snack at any time of the day. There are many ways you can vary this dish and it's fun experimenting.

To serve 4
4 slices of wholemeal bread, crusts removed
4 eggs
4 slices of smoked ham or thick slices of smoked bacon
Oil for frying
Salt & freshly ground black pepper

Fry the slices of bread in oil until dark brown and crispy, remove and keep warm. Cut the ham or bacon to fit the fried bread and fry briefly in the oil. Place a slice or more of the ham or bacon on each piece of bread and keep warm. Crack each egg into a mug or small cup and slide it into the hot oil. Deep fry until golden, remove with a slotted spoon and place on top of each portion. Season with salt and pepper and serve immediately.

Egg Tapenade

The word ' tapenade' derives from the French Provençal word, *tapeno* meaning Caper, on which the recipe is based. It can be made well in advance and stored in jars in the fridge. There is plenty of scope for individualising.

To serve 6
6 hard-boiled eggs
1 tin of anchovy fillets
2 tbsp. capers
3 oz tinned tuna (optional)
24 black olives, stoned
Squeeze of lemon juice
2 or 3 drops of chilli sauce
Olive oil
Salt & pepper

Cut the eggs in half, lengthways and remove the yolks. Pound together, the capers, tuna, olives and anchovy fillets to make the tapenade and mix in the egg yolks. Season with the chilli sauce, lemon juice and salt and pepper and as much olive oil as needed to form a paste. Spoon the mixture into the white egg cavities and serve on a platter with a tiny sprig of parsley on each.
As an alternative - mix the egg yolks with a desert spoon or two of Greek yoghurt, a teaspoon of curry powder, season and stuff the cavities with the mixture and decorate with an anchovy fillet.

Baked Eggs (Eggs en Cocotte)

This has to be one of the simplest starters ever.
It matters, however, that the eggs are cooked just
right, if they are allowed to become hard-baked the
dish becomes rather unpalatable.

To serve in 6 ramekins
6 fresh eggs
Tomato sauce
Double cream
Salt & freshly ground black pepper

Place a dash of tomato sauce to cover the bottom of each ramekin. Cover with a thin layer of double cream. Break an egg into each ramekin and place them on an oven tray in a hot oven for 3 or 4 minutes until the egg white firms. Serve immediately, dusted with salt and pepper and a slice or two of buttered bread.

Jason's Eggs Benedict

Our son, a chef in Sydney, contributed this recipe which has become
a family favourite. It goes down well at breakfast or as a light snack
during the day - even the sort of thing eaten by 'ladies who lunch'!

To serve 4
4 eggs
2 thin slices of smoked ham, cut into ribbons [Black Forest ham is ideal]
4 English muffins
For the hollandaise sauce
1/2 lb. unsalted butter
3 egg yolks
Juice of half lemon
Salt & pepper
2 tsp. warm water

To make the hollandaise sauce - melt the butter, place the egg yolks in a bowl with the lemon juice and whisk in a bain-marie over a pan of hot water until it thickens and doubles in size. Slowly add the butter in a trickle, whisking continuously. When half the butter has been added, test for flavour and, if required, add a little more lemon juice and then the rest of the butter. If the sauce becomes too thick, add a teaspoon or two of water. Season and keep warm.
Poach the eggs and keep them warm in a bowl of warm water. Cut the muffins in half, scoop out most of the centre of one half and toast both halves lightly. Place a poached egg in each hole and spread a few ribbons of ham over each egg and cover with some of the hollandaise sauce. Balance the top of each muffin by the side of each portion and serve whilst warm.

Courgette Soufflé

Making soufflés for a large dinner party is usually a recipe for disaster, however, for a supper for six this recipe should present no problem.

To serve 6
6 ramekins
1 1/2 lb. fresh courgettes
2 oz. butter
1 oz. flour
4 fl oz. milk
2 egg yolks
4 egg whites
2 oz. Parmesan cheese, grated
Salt & white pepper

Use some of the butter to grease the ramekins. Slice 1 lb. of courgettes and sprinkle with salt in a colander. Chop the remaining 1/2 lb into 1/4 inch cubes and sprinkle with salt. Leave both for about an hour, then rinse and pat them dry on kitchen paper. Put the sliced courgettes into a saucepan with a drop of salted water and cook until tender, drain and blend until smooth. Melt the butter in a saucepan, stir in the flour to make a paste and add the milk, drop by drop. Mix in the courgette mixture and cook on moderate heat, stirring constantly until the mixture begins to thicken. When the mixture has cooled, add the cheese and egg yolks and whisk well. Season and leave the mixture to stand for an hour or so or until you are ready to cook. Fry the cubed courgettes in a small amount of butter until well browned. Drain on kitchen paper. Whisk the egg whites until stiff and gradually fold it all into the mixture. Spoon the soufflé mixture into the ramekins up to half way and add a teaspoon of the cubed courgette to each. Cover with the remaining soufflé mixture and place each ramekin in a roasting tin. Pour in boiling water, up to half way up the ramekins and bake in a hot oven for 20 minutes or until they have risen. Remove from the oven and serve at once.

Poached Eggs in Jelly

This simple starter should be prepared with very fresh eggs, if you can get your hands on them. The stock can be made in advance unless, like me, you cheat and dissolve a chicken stock cube in a pint or two of boiled water and add gelatine because there is no time to make stock.

To serve 8
8 fresh eggs
Carcass and skin of one chicken, including wing tips and feet, if attached
2 oz. pork or bacon rinds
1 onion stuck with cloves
1 carrot, roughly chopped
3 cloves garlic, peeled
1 bouquet garni
Salt
1 or 2 thinly sliced olives for decoration
Lettuce, finely sliced for garnish

Break up the chicken carcass as much as possible and place in a large stockpot, cover with water and bring to the boil. Continually skim off any scum that comes to the surface. Add the remaining ingredients apart from the eggs, season with salt and place in a slow oven or on low heat for 5 or 6 hours. Strain the stock through fine muslin and allow to cool. Place in the fridge overnight until the stock has set firmly, then skim off the layer of fat that will have risen to the surface and wipe the surface with a damp cloth to remove all traces of fat. At this point check that the stock is firm enough to keep its shape. If in doubt, heat it and add some gelatine.
Spoon a thin layer of the stock into the bottom of each mould or ramekin and put them in the fridge for 10 minutes or so to set. Lay a slice of olive in the centre of each mould and pour a thin layer of stock over the slices and again, place the moulds in the fridge to set. Gently, poach the eggs in small batches until the white is cooked but the yolk is still runny. Slide the poached eggs into a shallow dish of cold water to stop further cooking. Trim the egg whites with a knife to a size and shape to fit the moulds and lay them, yolk side down, into each mould. Fill each mould with the remaining stock and return them to the fridge to set. When ready to serve the dish, spread each plate with a portion of the chopped lettuce, run the tip of a sharp knife around the moulds, gently shake out the jellied egg onto the palm of your hand and slip them onto the lettuce on the plate and serve.

Pakura

Small balls of deep fried chopped vegetables make an interesting starter for a light meal or as accompaniment to a pre-dinner aperitif. Like onion bhaji, they take some time to prepare but are easy to cook.

To serve 4
1 potato, peeled and cut into tiny dice
2 onions, cut into very fine dice
1 green pepper, core removed and cut into fine dice
1 red or green hot chilli, seeded and cut into fine dice
1/2 tsp. each, ground cumin and turmeric powder
1 handful, chopped fresh coriander
1 egg, lightly whipped
Oil for frying
5 oz. seasoned flour
Salt & freshly ground black pepper

Place all the ingredients, except the coriander, in a bowl, season well and add sufficient water to make a stiff paste. Heat the oil in a deep fat fryer and spoon in table tennis sized balls of the mixture. Fry for 10 minutes or so until the balls turn golden brown, drain thoroughly on kitchen paper, season and serve warm with a slice of lemon or lime and a sprinkling of chopped coriander.

Stuffed Aubergine (Imam Bayeldi)

Imam Bayeldi is a famous Turkish speciality. When translated, the name means '*The Imam fainted*' although why it should have been called that is not entirely clear. Some say it is because a Turkish priest fainted when told how much olive oil was used to make it. It is easy to prepare and is best served as a starter, cold or lukewarm.

To serve 6
6 medium sized aubergine
2 large onions, finely sliced
1/4 pint. olive oil
2 tsp. sugar
Juice of one lemon
3 large garlic cloves, crushed
4 large tomatoes, peeled, seeded and chopped
1 bunch parsley, chopped
Salt

The aubergine can be prepared in two or three different ways. My suggestion is that you cut off a half inch slice at the stalk end, just below the hull and reserve them to use as corks. Scoop out the pulp with a spoon or small sharp knife being careful not to pierce the skin. Sprinkle the inside of each shell, liberally, with salt and leave them, inverted in a colander to drain for at least forty minutes.

Fry the onion and sugar in some oil until soft but don't allow the onion to change colour, then add the garlic and simmer for ten minutes or so. Remove from the heat, stir in the parsley and chopped tomatoes, season, mix well and set aside.

Rinse the aubergine shells in cold water to remove any surplus salt, dry and stuff them with the cooled tomato mixture. Add a drop or two of water to the mixture if it appears a bit too dry. Place the reserved 'corks' on each aubergine and pack them, close together, in a suitable lidded oven dish. Pour over the remaining olive oil, season with salt and lemon juice and a little water, cover with a tightly fitting lid and bake in a medium oven for 40 minutes or until the aubergines are very soft.

Roasted Stuffed Bell Peppers

To serve 6
3 large bell peppers
18 ripe, cherry tomatoes
2 oz. tin, anchovy fillets
4 cloves garlic, thinly sliced
6 tbsp. Parmesan, grated
Olive oil
Red wine vinegar
Salt and freshly ground black pepper

Halve the peppers from top to bottom through the stalk and remove seeds and any pith. Oil the base of an ovenproof dish and lay the pepper halves in it, skin side down. Cut the tomatoes in half and place three halves in each pepper, scatter over some garlic slices and season well. Place one or two anchovy fillets over the tomatoes, a drizzle of vinegar and a splash of oil. Shake a tablespoon of grated Parmesan over each and bake in a hot oven for thirty or forty minutes until the cheese has melted and the pepper is tender and ready to eat.

Sherry

Sherry, the best known fortified wine in Spain, gets its name from the town of Jerrez de la Frontera in Andalucia. The most common grape varieties used to make it are Palomino, sometimes called Listan, and Pedro Ximenez. The whole process of producing sherry is done in *bodegas* (wine stores) using the *solera* system. The raw wine is allowed to ferment like any other wine and develop a bacterial growth on the surface called *flor*. It is then stored in oak barrels, fortified by brandy and matured for several years. The secret is in the blending of various wines from casks of many different varieties and ages and each establishment makes sherries of differing flavour and strength. There are basically four types of sherry, fino, manzanilla, amontillado and oloroso. In Spain it is possible to buy sherry so lightly fortified with brandy that it is enjoyed throughout a meal like any other wine.

A SELECTION of TAPAS

The custom of nibbling these small delicacies to accompany apéritifs, particularly in the evening, is widespread in Spanish bars and restaurants. Tapas have become so popular that they can sometimes take the place of a full dinner. There are a great many different kinds and may include dishes made with meat, fish, cheese, eggs or vegetables. Some are light and spicy, others, like sautéed kidneys and pigs trotters, can be quite substantial. In Spain they are served in small earthenware dishes or bowls and are eaten with the fingers or with wooden cocktail sticks.

Escalivada (Roasted vegetable salad)

To serve 4
2 green peppers
2 red peppers
1 aubergine,
2 shallots, peeled
2 tomatoes
2 1/4 tbsp. olive oil
3/4 tbsp. white wine vinegar
4 slices wholemeal bread, toasted, crusts removed
Salt & freshly ground black pepper

Place all the vegetables in an oven dish, sprinkle with olive oil and roast in a hot oven for about 1 hour. Peel and seed the peppers and cut them into strips. Place in a mixing bowl. Cut the aubergine into cubes and quarter the tomatoes, add to the bowl. Add the rest of the oil and the vinegar. Season with sea salt and black pepper and mix well. Chill and leave to marinate for at least 6 hours. Serve on the toast.

Champinones a la Plancha (Grilled Mushrooms)

To serve 4
4 large field mushrooms, stems removed
1 garlic clove, finely chopped
Olive oil
1 tbsp. chopped parsley
Salt & freshly ground black pepper

Season the mushrooms and sprinkle with garlic. Lightly coat with olive oil and cook in a heavy pan over high heat until done (about 3 min. per side). Serve, chopped into quarters on small plates with a drizzle of olive oil and the parsley.

Fried Prawn with Garlic

To serve 4
1 1/2 tbsp. vegetable oil
6 cloves garlic, peeled and finely sliced
24 fresh or defrosted prawns, shelled and deveined
1/2 tbsp. chilli powder
1 tbsp. finely chopped fresh thyme
Salt and freshly ground black pepper

Heat the oil in a saucepan, add the garlic and fry until the slices begin to turn golden. Remove with a slotted spoon and drain on paper towel. Season the prawns and dust with the chilli powder. Cook in the garlic-flavoured oil until they turn pink, about 2 or 3 minutes. Remove the prawns with a slotted spoon and place in a mixing bowl. Add the thyme, sprinkle with the reserved garlic chips and serve in small dishes or bowls with slices of French bread to soak up the juices.

Fried Squid with Anchovy Dressing

To serve 8
Anchovy dressing:
1 tbsp. Hellmann's mayonnaise
2 fl oz white wine vinegar
8 fl oz olive oil
2 oz. tin anchovy fillets
1 shallot, coarsely chopped
3 tbsp. parsley, finely chopped
2 garlic cloves, finely chopped
2 tbsp. fresh lime or lemon juice
For the squid
3 tbsp. flour
6 fl oz. water
8 squid, cleaned and sliced into rings
Salt & freshly ground black pepper
Vegetable oil for frying

Combine all the dressing ingredients in a blender and blend until smooth. Season with salt and pepper. In a small mixing bowl, whisk together the flour and water until smooth. The batter should be just thick enough to adhere to the squid, season with salt and pepper to taste. Heat oil in a large saucepan to 375 degrees F. Season squid with salt and pepper and dip into the batter. Remove the rings of squid with a slotted spoon, allowing any excess batter to drip off. Deep fry the squid until crisp on all sides and golden brown, remove and drain on paper towels. Serve on small plates with the anchovy dressing.

Tortilla de Patata (Spanish Potato Omelette)

To serve 4
3 tbsp. olive oil
2 lbs. potatoes, peeled and sliced into 1/8 inch slices
1 large onion, thinly sliced
Sea salt and freshly ground black pepper
4 large eggs

Heat the oil in a deep pan, add the sliced onion and fry until translucent. Add the slices of potato, one at a time to avoid sticking. Cook slowly over medium heat, turning the potatoes until tender. Allow the potato slices to break up slightly as they cook. Drain away surplus oil. Beat the eggs in a bowl until slightly foamy and add salt to taste. Pour the egg mixture over the onions and potatoes and press down to cover. When the bottom is brown, cover the pan with a plate, turn the pan up side down and remove the tortilla. Return, uncooked side down, by sliding the tortilla into the pan and cook the other side. Turn several times until cooked. Remove from the pan and cut into 1 inch squares. Serve with cocktail sticks.

Albondigas Caseras (Meatballs)

To serve 4 or 6
1 1/2 lb. minced beef
1/2 lb. minced pork
3 tbsp. bread crumbs
5 cloves garlic, minced
2 eggs
1/2 tsp. ground nutmeg
2 tsp. salt
3/4 tsp. freshly ground pepper
Flour for dusting
3 tbsp. olive oil
1 medium onion, coarsely chopped
1 green bell pepper, cut in 1/4 inch strips
1 small tomato, skinned and coarsely chopped
4 fl oz. dry white wine
6 fl oz. chicken stock
Salt and freshly ground pepper

In a mixing bowl, combine the minced beef and pork with bread the crumbs, 4 cloves of garlic, the eggs, nutmeg, salt, and pepper. Form into small balls the size of quail eggs and dust with flour. Sauté the meatballs in a casserole in oil until well browned on all sides and set aside. Add the onion, the remaining garlic and green pepper to the casserole and cook until the onion becomes opaque. Add the tomato, wine and chicken stock, season well and simmer, covered, for 30 minutes. Return the meatballs to the casserole and cook for a further 15 minutes. Serve on small plates or bowls.

Spiced Chorizo Sausage with Figs

To serve 4 - 6
4 chorizo sausages (1 lb) cut into 1 inch pieces
8-10 dried figs, halved
1 small onion, thinly sliced
1 tbsp. olive oil
4 fl oz. red wine
1 level tbsp. sugar
4 fl oz. red wine vinegar
1 stick cinnamon
A pinch of ground cloves

Heat the oil in a heavy-bottomed pan and lightly brown the chorizo. Add remaining ingredients and simmer gently for 30 minutes. Divide into 4 equal portions in small bowls and serve with crusty bread.

Salt Cod Fritters

To serve 4
1/2 lb. salt cod, skinned, boned and roughly chopped
1 tbsp. flour
8 fl oz. milk
1 1/2 tbsp. olive oil
1 egg yolk
2 egg whites
1 garlic clove, crushed
1 tbsp. chopped parsley
Vegetable oil for frying
Salt & freshly ground black pepper

Soak the salt cod overnight in plenty of cold water. Drain, replace with fresh water and bring to the boil. Reduce heat and simmer for 30 - 40 minutes. Remove any froth which forms on the surface, drain and mash the fish to a paste. Blend the mashed cod with the oil and flour in a bowl, together with the milk and lightly beaten egg yolk. Add the crushed garlic and the chopped parsley, season with a little salt and pepper and mix thoroughly. Beat the egg whites until stiff and fold into the cod paste immediately before cooking. Form the paste into small flat rounds and deep fry in very hot oil. Wait until they rise to the surface and turn light golden brown. Remove with a slotted spoon leave on paper towels to drain. Serve on individual small saucers.

Stuffed Cherry Tomatoes

8 - 10 servings
4 heaped tbsp. green Spanish olives with pimento
1 1/2 tsp. capers
1 tsp. brandy
1/4 tsp. freshly grated lemon zest
2 tbsp. extra-virgin olive oil
Salt & freshly ground black pepper
32 small cherry tomatoes
Chopped fresh parsley for garnish

In a food processor, pulse the olives until chopped fine. Add the remaining ingredients except the tomatoes and parsley and pulse to form a firm paste. With a sharp knife, slice the stem end from each tomato and discard. Using a thin teaspoon, remove the juice and seeds from each tomato, leaving the outside shell intact. Spoon a generous teaspoon of the tapenade into each shell and garnish with the parsley. Divide into 8 or 10 portions and serve on small saucers.

Steamed Mussels

To serve 8 - 10
2 lbs. mussels, cleaned
1/4 tsp. ground turmeric
2 fl oz dry white wine
1 onion, finely chopped
2 oz. thickly-sliced smoked ham, chopped fine
1/2 red bell pepper, chopped fine
1/2 green bell pepper, chopped fine
3 tbsp. olive oil
2 garlic cloves, minced
1lb. tin plum tomatoes, drained and chopped

Place the cleaned mussels in a large heavy-bottomed pot and pour in 6 fl oz. of boiling water. Cover with a lid and steam them for about 3 minutes or until mussels open. Remove from heat and allow to cool. Transfer the mussels with a slotted spoon to a bowl, reserving the liquid, and strain the liquid through a fine sieve into another small bowl. Cook the onion, chopped ham, and bell peppers in some oil over moderate heat, stirring, until the vegetables are softened, add the garlic, and cook the mixture, stirring, for a minute or so. Add the tomatoes and continue to cook, stirring constantly, for 5 minutes, or until it begins to thicken. Add the turmeric and reserved mussel liquid and boil the mixture until most of the liquid has evaporated. Season with salt and pepper and let it cool to room temperature. While the sauce is cooling discard the top shell from each mussel and loosen the mussels from the bottom shells. Arrange the half shells on a platter and cover with the sauce.

Seasoned Carrots with Herbs

To serve 8 - 10
4 large cloves garlic
1/2 tsp. dried oregano
3/4 tsp. cumin seeds
1 tsp. ground coriander
1/2 tsp. chopped red chilli
3 tbsp. red wine vinegar
4 fl oz. olive oil, for the dressing, plus 2 tbsp. for carrots
2 lbs. tender young carrots cut into 1/2 inch slices on the diagonal
8 fl oz water
Pinch of sugar
1/2 tsp. each, salt and freshly ground black pepper
Small bunch flat-leaf parsley, finely chopped

Combine the garlic, oregano, cumin seeds, coriander, and chilli pepper in a blender. Add the vinegar and blend to a paste. Drizzle in the olive oil in a thin stream and blend until the mixture thickens. In a heavy-bottomed saucepan, heat the olive oil over medium heat and add the carrots. Fry for 3 or 4 minutes, stirring occasionally, until they begin to soften. Add the water, sugar (if desired), salt, and pepper and cover. Reduce the heat and cook, shaking the pan occasionally, for about 5 more minutes, or until the carrots are just tender but not mushy. Add a little more water if necessary. Transfer the carrots to a serving bowl with a slotted spoon and immediately add the herb dressing. Toss together, cool and cover the bowl with plastic wrap. Leave the carrots to marinate for 2 to 3 hours, and when ready to serve, stir in the parsley. Serve at room temperature on tiny plates or ramekins.

Pinchitos Morunos (Moorish Kebabs)

To serve 4
1 lb. pork, cubed
1/2 tsp. thyme
1 tsp. cumin
1/2 tsp. paprika
1 bay leaf, crumbled
1 tbsp. chopped parsley
1 tsp. chopped chilli pepper
4 fl oz. olive oil

Rub the meat with the marinating spices and the olive oil, Cover and marinate a few hours or overnight in the refrigerator. Place the meat on skewers and grill over high heat until cooked through. Divide onto 4 small plates and serve with toothpicks.

Baked Squid

To serve 4 - 6
2 fl oz. olive oil
1 small onion, finely chopped
1 tbsp. garlic, finely chopped
2 fl oz. green Spanish olives, pitted, and chopped
1/4 tsp. powdered turmeric
1 tbsp. tomato paste
4 fl oz. dry white wine
4 fl oz. fish stock
1 lb. baby squid, cut into rings, tentacles cut in half
Salt & freshly ground black pepper

Heat the olive oil in a small casserole and fry the onion slowly until transparent. Add the garlic and olives and cook for a couple of minutes. Stir in the turmeric, tomato paste, wine and fish stock. Simmer for about five minutes to bring out the flavour before pouring the whole mixture into a preheated earthenware dish. Stir in the squid and put the dish into a hot oven for 35 to 40 minutes. Remove from the oven, taste and adjust the seasoning. Serve with bruschetta.

Bruschetta to accompany the squid
Stick of French bread cut into one inch slices
1 clove garlic, cut in half
2 fl oz. extra virgin olive oil
1 very ripe tomato, cut in half
Salt & freshly ground black pepper

Rub the bread with the garlic to lightly flavour it. Brush the bread with olive oil and toast in the oven or on a barbecue. Rub the toasted bread with the inside flesh of the tomato and serve with the baked squid.

Stuffed New Potatoes

To serve 4 - 6
12 new potatoes, well scrubbed
2 large eggs
2 tbsp. mayonnaise
1/2 tsp. garlic, finely chopped
1 tsp. parsley, finely chopped
2 tbsp. red onion, finely chopped
1oz. salmon eggs

Bring the potatoes to the boil in salted water and simmer until they are just cooked. Hard-boil the eggs in a different saucepan. Cool both potatoes and eggs in ice-cold water and pat dry. Using a sharp knife, cut off both ends of the potatoes so they will stand up. Using a small melon baller or teaspoon, scoop out the centre of the potatoes, leaving about a 1/8-inch shell, reserving the potato scraps. Peel and chop the eggs. In a mixing bowl, combine the reserved potato scraps, chopped eggs, mayonnaise, garlic, parsley, onions and season well. Fill each potato with a teaspoon of the mixture. Top each potato with some salmon eggs and garnish with parsley.

Patatas Con Alcaparras Y Eneldo
(Potatoes with Capers & Dill)

This makes an interesting variation on potato salad

To serve 4 - 6
1 1/2 lbs. potatoes
4 fl oz. olive oil
2 tbsp. fresh lemon juice
2 tbsp. orange juice
2 tbsp. onion, finely chopped
2 tbsp. parsley, finely chopped
1 tbsp. fresh dill, finely chopped
4 tsp. capers
Salt & freshly ground pepper
Fresh dill, for garnish

Boil the potatoes in their skins in salted water until tender. In a small bowl mix together the oil, lemon juice, orange juice, onion, parsley, dill, capers, salt, and pepper to make a dressing. Leave at room temperature for the flavours to mix. Drain the potatoes and allow them to cool. Skin them and cut into slices about 1/8 inch thick and arrange in layers in a serving dish. Pour some of the dressing over each layer and sprinkle with salt. Marinate for several hours at room temperature, carefully turning occasionally with a metal spatula. Serve at room temperature, decorated with a sprig of dill.

Carrot Salad

A quite different carrot salad with Middle Eastern overtones

To serve 4 - 6
1/2 lb. carrots, scraped and trimmed
8 fl oz. chicken stock
Salt & freshly ground black pepper
2 tbs. white wine vinegar
Water
2 large cloves garlic, put through a garlic press
1/4 tsp. dried oregano
1/4 tsp. freshly ground cumin
1/4 tsp. paprika

Bring the carrots to the boil in a mixture of 1/3 salted water and 2/3 chicken stock, reduce the heat and simmer for about 10 minutes until just cooked but still crisp. Remove the carrots with a slotted spoon, cool and cut into 1/4-inch slices. Mix together the vinegar, 2 tablespoons of the boiling liquid, garlic, oregano, cumin, paprika, and season with salt and pepper. Pour the dressing over the carrots, mix well and marinate overnight.

Fried Squid

To serve 4 - 6
4 oz. baby squid, cut into rings
2 tbsp. seasoned flour
Sea salt & freshly ground black pepper
1 egg
5 fl oz. milk
Vegetable oil for frying
Lemon wedges

Drop the squid rings in the seasoned flour in a bowl. Whisk the egg and milk together in a mixing bowl. Heat the oil in a heavy-based frying pan. Dip the floured squid rings, one at a time, into the egg mixture, shaking off any excess liquid and fry in the hot oil, in batches if necessary, for 2-3 minutes on each side until golden. Remove from the pan with a slotted spoon and dry on kitchen paper, sprinkle with salt and pepper and serve on small plates with the lemon wedges.

Chicken Balls

To serve 4 - 6
3 tbsp. flour
8 fl oz. milk
1 cooked chicken leg or thigh, skinned and de-boned
Pinch nutmeg
16 fl oz. olive oil
Salt & freshly ground black pepper
2 Eggs, beaten
3 tbsp. breadcrumbs

Finely mince the chicken in a processor. Sauté the meat in 2 tablespoons of olive oil. Mix half the flour in a little milk to form a runny paste. Heat the rest of the milk and when it's about to boil, add the milk paste. Keep stirring, constantly, with a wooden spoon to prevent the formation of lumps. Cook at low heat for about 10 minutes until the mixture begins to thicken. Season and add the nutmeg to taste. Add the chicken and stir for 3 to 5 minutes more, on low heat. Cool and form into small croquettes using two spoons or your hands. Dip, first in the remaining flour, then the beaten egg allowing the excess drip off, and finally coat with breadcrumbs. Fry the croquettes until golden brown in hot olive oil. Remove with a slotted spoon and drain on paper towels. Serve in small bowls.

Spinach Empanadas

The term empanada is used for any raw or cooked filling wrapped in pastry and baked in the oven or over an open fire. These pies are mentioned in culinary documents as far back as medieval times.

To serve 4 - 6
For the filling
1 1/2 lb spinach
3 fl oz. olive oil
4 cloves garlic, finely chopped
6 oz tomatoes, peeled and chopped
3 oz tinned tuna
2 tbsp. pine nuts
2 eggs, hardboiled and finely chopped
Salt & freshly ground black pepper
For the pastry
6 tbsp. flour
2 fl oz. olive oil
2 fl oz. milk
A few drops lemon juice
1/2 tbsp. baking powder
Salt
1 egg, beaten

Boil the spinach, in a minimum of water, for 10 minutes or until tender, drain and set aside. Sauté the garlic in the oil until golden, add the tomatoes. When the tomatoes begin to break-up, add the spinach, tuna and pine nuts. Simmer for 5 minutes, remove from the heat and add the chopped egg and season well. Put the flour in a bowl and add the oil, milk, lemon juice, baking powder and salt. Knead by hand until the dough comes away from the sides of the bowl. Leave to rest, covered in foil, for 20 minutes or so. When ready to cook, roll the dough into a thin sheet. Cut into 4-6 discs. Place a tablespoon of filling on each round. Fold over and seal the edges with a little water, making a narrow rim. Brush each with a little beaten egg and bake in a hot oven for approximately 30 minutes. Serve warm or cold.

Spicy Pork with Sherry Sauce

To serve 10 - 12
For marinade
4 fl oz. olive oil
2 fl oz. white wine vinegar
2 tbsp. parsley, finely chopped
1tsp. chopped dried chilli pepper
2 garlic cloves, crushed
1/2 tsp. ground cumin
1/2 tsp. ground coriander
1/2 tsp. cayenne
Salt & freshly ground black pepper
1 1/2 lbs. pork fillet, cut into 1/2 inch cubes

Combine all ingredients to make marinade. Add pork, cover and refrigerate for a minimum of 6 hours or overnight. Remove pork with a slotted spoon. Heat 2 tablespoons marinade in large pan over medium heat. Add pork in batches and cook until meat is well browned. Dry on kitchen paper and serve on a large dish with the dipping sauce.

Sherry Dipping Sauce
1 tbsp. marinade
1 tsp. flour
4 fl oz. sweet sherry
2 fl oz. water
Salt to taste

Heat the marinade in a saucepan over low heat. Sprinkle with flour until sauce thickens. Add sherry, water and salt to taste.

Red Peppers with Anchovies

To serve 4 - 6
2 large red bell peppers
4 garlic cloves, finely sliced
4 tbsp. olive oil
A 2oz. tin of anchovy fillets

Roast the peppers in a hot oven for 15 minutes. Cool, peel and seed the peppers and cut them into 1/2 inch wide strips. Heat the olive oil in a frying pan and fry the garlic until it begins to turn golden. Add the pepper strips and sauté for 5 minutes or so, shaking the pan from time to time. Drain the peppers, coil the anchovies around the strips and serve, cold or warm on small plates.

Scallop Ceviche

Scallops survive in great numbers off the coast of Galicia
in Spain where they are almost as popular as mussels.

To serve 4
16 scallops, cleaned with the beard and coral removed.
4 fl oz. fresh lemon juice
1 onion, finely chopped
1 tbsp. light soy sauce
Salt and freshly ground black pepper

Combine the lemon juice, onion and soy sauce to make a marinade. Add the scallops, mix well and refrigerate for about 30 minutes. Divide the scallops between 4 small bowls, drizzle a drop of the marinade over with a pinch of salt & pepper and serve.

Tortillitas de Camarones (Prawn Cakes)

To serve 4
2 tbsp. flour
2 large eggs
5 tbsp. water
1 bunch of spring onions, finely chopped
2 tbsp. parsley, finely chopped
1/2 lb. shelled prawns
Salt, pepper and paprika to taste
Vegetable oil for frying

Mix the flour and eggs in a mixing bowl. Add some water bit by bit and stir into a smooth batter. Add spring onions, parsley and prawns and season well. Let the mixture stand for an hour or more. Heat some oil in a frying pan. Spoon in about 2 tablespoons of the batter at a time, flatten with the back of the spoon into a thin pancake. Fry on each side until golden. Serve immediately.

Henri de Toulouse-Lautrec

Henri de Toulouse-Lautrec *and his great friend and trustee, Maurice Joyant, had known each other since childhood and apart from art, shared a fascination for beautiful women and good food. They spent years dreaming up exotic menus and recipes. Some time after Lautrec's death and shortly before his own, Joyant published a collection of recipes invented in Lautrec's company with many drawings and illustrations by the artist, as a tribute to his friend.*

Lautrec travelled all over Europe and wherever he went he sought out recipes and ideas for recipes which he then experimented with on his return, with his friend, Joyant. People were not surprised to be invited to dinner to eat kangaroo or elephant foot. The instructions might read, "First catch your elephant"!

Lautrec came from an aristocratic family who were keen foodies and always involved in the day to day decisions of the kitchen. They didn't rely, totally, on the efforts of their domestic staff.

Lautrec liked to organize his dinner parties down to the last detail and went to endless trouble to ensure that each gathering met with his approval. He even spent time designing and illustrating the menu cards as well as the invitations. He understood that small intimate supper parties were the best and regularly invited his artist and writer friends together with a few bourgeoisie and one or two from the aristocracy. He and his friends were free from most common forms of social prejudice and liked to mix the guests invited to their soirees.

He was a great gourmand and was known to carry a small grater with a nutmeg to flavour his food and the wine he drank. He loved dishes that had been simmered slowly for hours and were cleverly seasoned. Although he ate in taverns a great deal, he was also an accomplished cook who was not put off by complicated recipes.

In France, at this time, it was not uncommon for men like Lautrec to exchange ideas for recipes and to hold an intense interest in the preparation of food. They considered cuisine to be a matter worthy of man's artistic interest, a subject not to be left to the competence of their wives alone.

His recipes, however, were brief in the extreme and assumed that the reader had a good knowledge of the art of cooking. As an example, here is a recipe for squirrel, I don't know if he was being serious but this is what was said:-

> Having killed some squirrels in autumn, skin them the same day and empty them. Roll them up in a piece of lard and let them brown with some good quality butter in a copper saucepan. When they are a good golden colour, salt them, cover, and let them cook on a very gentle fire. One must use no spice of any kind which might entail the risk of taking away from the animal its exquisite nutty flavour.

Marcus Aurelius Antoninus, Emperor of Rome

Aurelius Antoninus, *generally known to the world as* Heliogabalus, *became Emperor at 14 and died, probably murdered by the Praetorian Guard, aged 18. Little detail is known of his political or public life but his extraordinary feasts and orgies, many of which lasted for days, were notorious. He insisted that the couches on which he and his guests lay and all the utensils in his kitchens and at the table were made of solid silver. He devised a feast, lasting the whole day, whereby he and his courtiers travelled around the city, eating one course after another in a different house in turn. He was known to eat cock's-combs taken from living birds and the tongues of peacocks and nightingales because he was told that they would provide immunity from the plague.*

He served his guests huge platters heaped with flamingo-brains, thrush-brains and the heads of parrots and peacocks. On one occasion he is known to have ordered 600 ostrich brains to be prepared for a meal.

He fed his dogs goose-livers, sent grapes to his stables for his horses and fed parrots and pheasants to his pet lions. For ten successive days he served his guests peas with gold-pieces, lentils with onyx, beans with amber and rice with pearls. Had he survived to manhood there is no telling what other extravagances he might have indulged.

A SELECTION of MEZZE

A selection of spicy snacks, common to North Africa as well as the Middle East and Eastern Europe, is usually served cold to accompany a glass or three of strong liquor. The list of possible dishes is long but I have chosen a selection that is both simple to make, delicious to eat and common to most of those countries. A selection of only one or two of these dishes might be chosen as a first course for a meal in the West whereas a wider choice might make up a complete dinner. To accompany a large meal it would be wise to ensure that the portions of mezze are kept small, otherwise people might lose their appetite before the main course is served. Creamed salads such as, hummus, tahina and aubergine puree should be served with strips of raw vegetables, such as green or red peppers, celery sticks or pieces of dry bread. Sometimes, small exact replicas of main dishes of fish, meat and chicken are produced such as fried or raw chicken livers, fried cubes of lamb, chicken or meat balls and miniature savoury pastries or pies. Bowls of fresh raw vegetables as well as pickles, olives and nuts, might be placed around the table.

Fried Liver

It is most important that these small chunks of liver are cooked quickly, crisp on the outside but still slightly pink in the centre. They are best served warm, straight from the pan.

To serve 4 - 6
4 lamb's livers
2 tbsp. olive oil
1 tbsp. white wine vinegar
1 small onion, finely sliced
1 tsp. each ground cumin, coriander, paprika
Juice of half a lemon
Salt & freshly ground black pepper

Cut the livers into 3/4 inch pieces, remove all sinews and place in a shallow bowl. Mix together the olive oil, vinegar, salt and pepper to make a marinade. Pour the mixture over the livers and leave to marinate for a couple of hours. When ready to cook, dry the livers on some kitchen paper and fry them quickly in very hot oil for a few moments, gently shaking the pan to prevent the pieces sticking to the bottom. Drain and serve warm on small plates, sprinkled with lemon juice and garnished with thinly sliced onion. Place the ground cumin, coriander and paprika in piles on a small plate and dip the pieces of liver in one or other spice. In some top Lebanese restaurants, thin slices of raw lamb's liver is substituted but it must be absolutely fresh.

Tabbouleh

Tabbouleh, a simple cracked wheat salad, is a Lebanese speciality served as a cold entrée or mezze in all Middle Eastern restaurants.

To serve 4
6 oz. bulgur wheat
1 lb. ripe tomatoes, finely diced
1 onion, finely diced
1 handful of fresh mint, finely chopped
1 handful of flat-leafed parsley, finely chopped
4 fl oz. extra virgin olive oil
1 tbsp. freshly squeezed lemon juice
Salt & freshly ground black pepper
3 spring onions, finely sliced

Soak the bulgur wheat in sufficient boiling water to cover for five or ten minutes to moisten the wheat. Drain away any surplus water and place the wheat in a mixing bowl. Stir in all the ingredients except the spring onions, season and mix well. Leave in a cool place for 2 or 3 hours, turning the mixture over occasionally. Serve on a flat dish garnished with spring onions.

Hummus bi Tahina

Hummus, a puréed chickpea salad, common throughout the Arab world can be adapted as a simple starter for any meal.

To serve 4
7oz. cooked chickpeas
2 tbsp. tahina paste
Juice 2 lemons
3 cloves garlic, peeled & crushed
1 tsp. ground cumin
Salt to taste
Cayenne pepper, parsley and a drop or two of olive oil for garnish

Rinse the chickpeas and place in a blender with the tahina paste, lemon juice, garlic, salt and the ground cumin. Blend to a smooth paste adding a drop or two of water if required. Pour the purée, which should have the consistency of thick cream, into a shallow bowl. Mix a little cayenne with some olive oil and dribble some over the surface of the purée. Scatter a few whole chickpeas over the surface and sprinkle with some chopped parsley. Serve with pitta, or crusty French bread.

Falafel

These bean rissoles are considered one of Egypt's national dishes. They are eaten for breakfast, lunch or dinner and have been a staple mezze dish for more than a thousand years. They are traditionally made with dried broad beans found in all Oriental and Indian stores and most delicatessens, however, chickpeas could be substituted. A dry falafel 'ready-mix' is also now available in many delicatessens but it doesn't beat the real thing.

To serve 10 - 12
1 lb. large preferably skinless, dried broad beans
1 onion, finely chopped
4 spring onions, finely chopped
6 garlic cloves, skinned and crushed
2 tsp. ground cumin
2 tsp. ground coriander
Handful each, flat leafed parsley and coriander, finely chopped
1 tsp. baking powder
1/2 tsp. cayenne pepper
Salt

If dried broad beans are used they should be soaked in cold water for at least 24 hours. (Chickpeas would not require soaking). Drain the broad beans and remove the skins, if this has not already been done, and leave the beans to dry in a colander. Place them in a food processor with the rest of the ingredients and blend to a very smooth paste. Allow the paste to rest for an hour or so. Heat about an inch of vegetable oil in a heavy-bottomed pan and form the paste into walnut sized lumps, flatten slightly and ease them carefully, a few at a time, into the hot oil. Deep-fry until they turn golden. Remove with a slotted spoon and drain on kitchen paper. Serve warm with pitta bread.

Dolmas

Dolmas are popular in all Middle Eastern countries. They are not exclusively rice-filled vine leaves. The Turks stuff a variety of other vegetables with a mixture of rice or meat. I have given the most typical recipe for stuffing vine leaves but it is also fun to experiment using the same stuffing with red or green peppers, courgettes or baby marrows.

To serve 4 - 6 with hot dolmas with meat based stuffing
20 preserved vine leaves
5 shallots, finely chopped
2 cloves garlic, crushed
1 tbsp. pine kernels
A small handful each of finely chopped parsley and mint
1 lb. minced lamb
4 oz short grain rice
Olive oil for cooking
Juice of one lemon
Salt & pepper

Soak the vine leaves in boiling water for 20 minutes to soften, remove excess salt and pat dry. Fry the shallots in the oil until soft, add the garlic, pine kernels, parsley, mint and lamb and stir-fry. When the lamb has begun to change colour add the rice, 10 fl oz of water and the lemon juice. Simmer for 20 minutes until the rice and lamb are almost cooked and the water has been absorbed. Check seasoning. Allow to cool then place the vine leaves, shiny side down, on a board, place two teaspoons of the mixture in the centre of each leaf and roll half-way up then fold in the sides and continue rolling into a small neat parcel. Place some leftover vine leaves in the bottom of a casserole and lay in the dolmas tight together, interspersed with garlic cloves. Sprinkle with lemon juice, add 2 fl oz of salted water and simmer in the oven for about half an hour. Serve warm.

For cold dolmas without meat, using leftover rice
1/2 lb. cooked rice
3 tomatoes, skinned and chopped
1/2 tsp. each cinnamon & ground allspice
1 handful each chopped mint and parsley
1 onion, finely chopped
1 clove garlic
Juice of half a lemon
1 tsp. sugar
Salt & pepper
Olive oil

Fry the onion in the oil to a pale gold colour. Add to the remaining ingredients and when the mixture has cooled wrap it, a teaspoon at a time, in the vine leaves as described above. Place the parcels tightly together in a casserole, cover with chicken or vegetable stock and simmer in a slow oven for about an hour. Cool, sprinkle with olive oil and serve.

Kibbeh [Minced Stuffed Lamb Balls]

This recipe from the Lebanon takes a bit of time to prepare but is easy to cook. You can experiment with the ingredients for the stuffing, but I have given a basic one popular throughout the Middle East, the ingredients for which are easily obtained in most supermarkets or delicatessens. In all parts of the Middle East, the preparation of these little dumplings is thought to be the standard by which women of the household are judged. Guests would be able to judge the refinement and skill of the wife by the quality of the kibbeh she served even if it was her cook who made them.

To serve 4 [3 kibbehs each]
For the stuffing
6 oz lean lamb, minced
1 small onion, finely chopped
1 level tsp. each, ground allspice & cinnamon
2 oz pine nuts, lightly toasted
1 handful coriander, roughly chopped
Olive oil
1/2 glass water
Sea salt & freshly ground black pepper
For the casing
9 oz lean lamb, finely minced
5 oz fine bulgur wheat, washed
1/2 small onion, grated
Sea salt & freshly ground black pepper

To make the stuffing, fry the onion until well browned, add the lamb, spices and stir, ensuring the lamb is well broken up. Add a little water, season with salt and pepper and simmer until the water has evaporated. Place the meat in a bowl and stir in the pine nuts and coriander. Leave to cool slightly.
To make the casing, grind the well seasoned meat and the onion in a food processor with a little water to form a paste. Wash the bulgur wheat and blend into the meat mixture.
To form the kibbeh, wet your hands and take enough of the casing mixture to form a ball the size of a golf ball. Flatten the ball into an oval shape, make a hole in one end with a finger in order to hollow out the kibbeh, ensuring that the sides are as thin as possible. Fill the hollow with a teaspoon or so of the stuffing mixture and gently seal the opening, ensuring that the oval shape is re-formed. Continue with the rest of the mixture - you should have enough for twelve egg-shaped ovals. When you have used all the mixture and are ready to eat, fry the kibbeh in hot olive oil until well browned and firm to the touch. Serve with minted yoghurt and a green salad.

Savoury Pastries

Known as borek in Turkey, sambousak in Iran, pasteles in Salonika these delicious miniature pastries or pies can be served hot or cold but are best straight out of the oven. They can be made with bread dough or flaky pastry but I have chosen to make them with paper-thin filo pastry. They are popular throughout the Middle East as well as Greece and Turkey. The name is derived from the Greek *phyllo* and sheets of ready-made filo can be purchased in most supermarkets and delicatessens.

To serve 10 - 12 at a supper party
12 sheets of prepared filo
Melted butter
Meat filling
1 onion, finely chopped
2 tbsp. butter
1 lb. minced lean lamb
2 tbsp. pine nuts
1 tsp. ground cinnamon
1 tsp. ground cumin
Salt & freshly ground black pepper
Alternative Cheese filling
1 lb. feta cheese
1 tbsp. each chopped parsley, mint and chives
Freshly ground black pepper

For the meat filling, gently fry the onion in butter until it turns golden. Add the meat and fry until it changes colour, then add the pine nuts. Season with salt and pepper, stir in the ground cinnamon and cumin, continue to fry until the meat is cooked. Cut each of the filo sheets, lengthways, into four rectangular strips about three inches wide. Brush each strip with melted butter. Put a teaspoon of either the meat or cheese mixture at one end of the sheet close to an edge. Fold one corner over the filling to make a triangle, fold again and again until the whole strip is folded into a triangle. Repeat with all the strips until the filling is used up. Place the pastries on an oiled baking sheet, brush with butter and bake in a hot oven for 30 minutes or until crisp and golden. Serve immediately.

Boiled Carrot Salad

I have no idea what the Moroccan name for this salad is but I do know it is hot and spicy. It is beautiful to look at and best made with older carrots, as they tend to taste sweeter.

To serve 4 - 6
1 lb. carrots, peeled and chopped into large chunks
1 tsp. each paprika and cayenne pepper
3 tbsp. white wine vinegar
1 tsp. cumin seeds
4 tbsp. extra virgin olive oil
2 cloves garlic, crushed
1 tsp. ginger, crushed
1 tbsp. honey
Salt & freshly ground black pepper
A few black olives, stoned and cut in half for garnish

Boil the carrots in salted water until very tender. Drain and allow to cool slightly. Place in a blender together with the other ingredients except the olives and blend to as fine paste. Serve cold in a small bowl garnished with a few olives.

Steamed Mussels & Vegetable Stew

To serve 4 -6
24 large mussels
1 small onion, peeled and finely chopped
1 tbsp. olive oil
1 small carrot, peeled and finely diced
1 small potato, peeled and finely diced
1 short stick of celery, finely diced
1 tbsp. tomato concentrate
1/2 tbsp. sugar
1 tomato, skinned and finely chopped
1 tbsp. parsley, finely chopped
2 cloves garlic, finely chopped
Salt & freshly ground black pepper

Steam the mussels in a small amount of salted water until the shells open. Cool, remove the meat and discard the shells. Fry the onions in oil until they become opaque, add the diced carrots, potatoes and garlic and fry on low heat for five minutes or so. Add the remaining ingredients and simmer over low heat, stirring gently from time to time, until all the vegetables are cooked. Add the mussels and stir into the sauce, simmer for five more minutes, cool and serve in small saucers with a slice or two of French bread.

The History of Sake

Sake *as well as being a generic Japanese term for alcoholic drink, is wine made from fermented rice. It has been made and drunk in Japan for a thousand years and is closely tied to both the religious and social life of the people. There are many types and makes of sake but it is generally a colourless liquid served hot or cold and often drunk with beer as a chaser. The choice ranges from very sweet to very dry and some, such as mirin are golden brownish in colour and used for cooking whilst others like seishu, are usually drunk with a meal. It is an ideal accompaniment for sashimi and sushi and, in Japan, is drunk from tiny handmade pottery or china cups.*
Many small family firms and even Shinto Priests started opening breweries all over the country. In 1583, the Konishi family, for example, started brewing Sumi Sake, a clear high quality sake, at their first brewery in a small village in Itami which is still in use to this day. They have since become famous for the manufacture of one of Japan's most popular sake brands, **Shirayuki***.*

Alexandre Grimod de La Reyniere

Alexandre Balthazar Laurent Grimod de La Reyniere, *did not have an auspicious start in life. He was born in Paris in 1758, the son of a Tax Collector, whose own father had been a pork butcher in Paris. His mother, from a minor aristocratic family, rejected him at birth. Born disabled, with one hand shaped like a claw and the other the form of a goose's foot, he was thought unlikely to survive. He was christened and immediately passed into the care of servants who provided his initial education. At eleven, he was given a small annual allowance and sent to University, from whence he graduated as a lawyer. He developed into something of a character with a reputation as a gourmet with exquisite taste and an irreverent but charming sense of humour. He managed to escape the guillotine during the Revolution only because his opinions about food were valued by both Danton and Robespierre.*

He is credited with being the first French food commentator and critic. An early version of the Good Food Guide or Guide Michelin, maybe. He set up a jury of tasters who provided the first anecdotic and practical gastronomical guide of Paris. Their role was to award certificates to various chefs and restaurants. After a series of tastings their pronouncements could establish forever the reputation of a certain chef or restaurant or, indeed, ruin them. The jury published a series of pamphlets that contained summaries of his recommendations and copies became a must for every gourmand in Paris. Unfortunately, he was accused of "interested partiality" in some of his decisions when it became clear he was not above accepting the occasional back-hander.

The committee was disbanded and de La Reyniere returned to the law. He continued to host lavish lunches for his friends, however, and in the evenings was to be found dining in style at the better restaurants in Paris. He became well known for his amusing comments that endeared him to the public at large. Proclamations, such as "a fine sauce will make even an elephant or a grandfather palatable", kept him in the public eye.

He died in 1837, considered by some to be a bit of a rogue and by others of being completely mad, an impression he carefully nurtured throughout his life. His reputation as a renowned gourmet, however, was never disputed.

SUSHI

Sushi is vinegar-flavoured rice served, in various forms, with a selection of fresh fish, vegetables or shellfish. Its origins are lost in time. It has been suggested that many years ago the Japanese preserved fish by salting and packing it between layers of rice. The fish fermented naturally and, by the time it was eaten, it had developed a slightly acidic flavour. With advances in technology, for the storing and transportation of fresh fish, it became no longer necessary to preserve it in salt. People, however, had grown accustomed to the acidic taste so in place of salting, vinegar was added to the rice instead and in time *sushi*, as we know it, developed into a dish in it's own right.

The most common form of *sushi* today is *nigiri sushi*, (hand-formed sushi), a style first seen in the Tokyo area in the early 19th century, using fresh fish caught in Tokyo Bay. Even today this form of *sushi* is sometimes referred to as *Edo-mae-zushi* (Edo being Tokyo's former name). *Sushi* roll or *maki-zushi* is vinegared rice rolled up in a sheet of seaweed (*nori*), with a choice of various types of fish or vegetables in the centre. The Americans have introduced a few variations of their own which suit their taste, for example, California roll, which has the rice on the outside and various fillings and mayonnaise in the centre. Another simple variety is *tomaki-zushi* (roll-your-own *sushi*) which is ideal for a buffet style meal.

It is impossible to produce at home the vast selection of fish and other ingredients used in many Japanese *sushi* bars. It is possible, however, to buy good quality fresh fish such as salmon, scallops, salmon eggs, mackerel, tuna and squid from most superstores and fishmongers. Other ingredients, such as avocado pear, cucumber and spring onions are all freely available.

It's important to ensure that all equipment required to make *sushi* is on hand before starting to cook. The equipment and ingredients can be purchased in most superstores.

Equipment

A very sharp knife for cutting the fish
Bowl for mixing rice and vinegar
Makisu - Bamboo mat for *sushi* roll
Wood chopping board
Paper fan for cooling the rice

Basic Ingredients for all Sushi

Wasabi - Japanese horseradish
Nori - Prepared sheets of seaweed
Sushi-zu - Vinagared rice flavouring
Shoyu - Soy sauce
Shoga no Amazu-zuke - Pickled ginger
Kome - Sushi rice (US No 1 Extra Fancy)

Nori-maki (Sushi Roll)

Arguably the easiest sushi to make and certainly the easiest to eat. They can be eaten with your fingers or with wooden Japanese chopsticks (*Shojin-hashi*). The choice of filling is up to you and what's available, but the trick is to keep it simple. Never put sushi in the fridge, it will go hard!

To serve 4 people as a starter or as part of a Japanese meal
2 sheets nori
1 cup rice
1 1/4 cups water
2 tbsp. rice vinegar
2 tsp. sugar
1 tsp. salt
4 oz. fresh salmon or tuna, cut into thin 1/4"strips
1 tbsp. wasabi
Soy sauce

Rinse the rice quickly in cold water two or three times until the water becomes almost clear. Drain and leave to stand for 20 minutes or so. Place the rinsed rice and fresh water in a heavy pot, cover and bring to the boil. Reduce the heat and simmer for 15 minutes. Remove from the heat and allow it to stand, covered, for 10 minutes. Transfer the rice to a wooden or glass bowl, dissolve the salt and sugar in the vinegar, pour the mixture over the rice and mix well with a wooden spatula, being careful not to mash it. Cool to room temperature by fanning which helps remove any surplus moisture. Cover with a damp dishcloth to prevent the rice drying out too much. Cut each *nori* sheet in half, lengthways and place one bit on the bamboo mat, shiny side down. When cold, gently spread 1/4 of the rice onto the *nori* sheet leaving 1/2 inch clear along one side. Spread a small amount of *wasabi* in a line along the centre of the rice. Lay the strips of salmon, end to end, in a line along the centre of the rice, on top of the *wasabi*. Start rolling by lifting the mat and pressing the *nori* sheet into a roll. Repeat the process with each of the sheets and then, wet a sharp knife and cut the rolls, carefully, into four equal-sized pieces. Serve an equal number to each guest with a small saucer of soy sauce for dunking and a pinch of *wasabi*.
Alternatives. Instead of salmon, try using an equal amount of tuna or cucumber for the filling.

(Maki-zushi) California Roll

The Americans developed this variety of sushi and called it a California Roll. Apart from having the rice on the outside it also uses mayonnaise which would be unheard of in Japan. Restaurants such as ' Nobu' in London have created new and exciting varieties of sushi in recent years, combining flavours and ingredients the traditionalists would scoff at.

To serve 4
Prepare sushi rice as described in the previous recipe
2 sheets nori
1/2 avocado pear, peeled and sliced into 1/4 inch strips
2 inches of cucumber, quartered with pips removed
4 oz. fresh salmon or tuna, cut into thin pencil shapes
2 tbsp. mayonnaise
1 tbsp. wasabi
2 tsp. sesame seed
Soy sauce

Cover the bamboo mat with cling film to protect it. Place a sheet of *nori* on the mat, shiny side down. Spread half the rice onto the *nori*, leaving 1/4 inch on the edge nearest you, uncovered. Gently turn the *nori* sheet over and place the rice-covered side on the mat. Spread a spoon full of mayonnaise over the *nori* and thin line of *wasabi*. Place some fish in a line in the centre, end to end along the *nori*, together with a line of avocado and beside it a line of cucumber. Carefully lift the bamboo mat with your thumbs, holding the ingredients in place with you other fingers and roll the *nori* tightly. Press the ends of the rolls in with your fingers. Sprinkle the sesame seed over the roll, wet a sharp knife and cut it in half and each half into three, wetting the knife each time to avoid sticking.
Repeat the process with the second sheet. Arrange three slices on each plate with a small amount of *wasabi* and a ramekin or small saucer of soy sauce. Ask your guests to mix a little of the *wasabi* in the soy and dunk each slice in it.

(Temaki-zushi) Roll-Your-Own Sushi

This is an original help-yourself type of starter and is great fun at a small supper party. You can use salmon, tuna, baby squid, shrimp, or just strips of cucumber or avocado as fillings. A mix of crabmeat and mayonnaise could also be prepared and used as a filling.

To serve 4-6
Prepare sushi rice as described in the first recipe
10 sheets nori (more if necessary)
4 oz. raw tuna fillet, thinly sliced
4 oz. raw salmon fillet
2 inch piece cucumber, halved, deseeded and cut into 1/4" sticks
1 avocado, peeled and sliced into 1/4" sticks
Soy sauce
1 tbsp. wasabi

Place the sushi rice in a bowl in the centre of the table surrounded by smaller bowls containing the various fillings. Cut the *nori* sheets in half to form small rectangles. Place a tablespoon of sushi rice at one end of the *nori*, in your left hand, add a touch of *wasabi*, the filling of you choice and roll from left to right to form a cone. Dunk the end in a drop of soy sauce - simple!

BIBLIOGRAPHY

Robert J. Courtine, *Larousse Gastronomique*, (Paul Hamlyn 1988)
Yukiko Moriyama, *Japanese Cuisine for Everyone*, (Joie,Inc 1988)
Ben Schott, *Schott's Food & Drink Miscellany*, (Bloomsbury 2003)
Claudia Roden, *A New Book of Middle Eastern Food*, (Penquin 1986)
Henri de Toulouse-Lautrec, *The Art of Cuisine*, (Michael Joseph Ltd 1966)
Fergus Henderson, *Nose to Tail Eating*, *A Kind of British Cooking*, (Bloomsbury 1999)

FOOD SHOPS and SUPPLIERS

Vallebona
Unit 14, 59 Weir Road,
Wimbledon,
London SW19 8UG
Tel: 020 8944 5665

Suppliers of Sardinian Gourmet Food
Including sea urchin

The Dairy
The Square,
Chagford
Devon TQ13
Tel: 01647

Enormous selection of English cheeses

Martin's Seafresh
St. Columb Business Centre
Barn Lane
St. Columb Major
Cornwall TR9 6BU
Sales Tel: 0800 027 2066

The freshest fish in the West